Ex
Libris

Lowell R. Kantzer

Evangelism
for Tomorrow

By CHARLES B. TEMPLETON

HARPER & BROTHERS PUBLISHERS NEW YORK

Contents

PREFACE   vii

I.   AGAINST THIS BACKGROUND   3

II.   THE CONTEMPORARY OPPORTUNITY   19

III.   TOWARD A CONCEPT OF EVANGELISM   31

IV.   TOWARD A TOTAL WITNESS   49

V.   FROM SUCH TURN AWAY   63

VI.   SIGNS OF RESURGENCE   75

VII.   THE PULPIT IS THE KEY   93

VIII.   DIRECTION FOR TOMORROW   111

IX.   THE GOAL IS COMMITMENT   129

X.   RECKONING WITH THE EMOTIONS   145

XI.   THE INVITATION   163

v

Preface

THIS IS not a book on the history of evangelism or on evangelistic techniques; it is an attempt (deliberately cast in "layman's language") to examine the nature of the evangelistic task and to delineate some of the misconceptions which have bedeviled the Church in its attempt to "do the work of an evangelist." It is not simply a call to evangelism, for evangelism, per se, is not necessarily a good thing, and much that has been done in its name has been baneful. Many an "evangelist" has been like the man in the modern parable who went about carrying something very much like a lantern—except that it shed darkness. The failure of the Church in evangelism consists not only in that it has left undone those things it ought to have done, but that it has done those things it ought not to have done.

This book is a distillation from almost twenty years spent in the study and practice of evangelism. During these years the writer has preached in every major city in the United States and in thirteen other countries under such varied auspices as non-denominational, Fundamentalist sects and the National Council of the Churches of Christ in the U. S. A. These two decades encompass nine years in the pastorate, two years as Secretary of the Division of Evangelism of the Presbyterian Church (U. S. A.) and lectureships in most of the leading theological seminaries in the United States and Canada.

It has been my lot to preach to congregations of half a dozen in bleak, hinterlands churches and to throngs ranging upward to fifty thousand people in the great sports arenas of the nations. I have seen penitents respond by walking down aisles spread with sawdust and by bowing their heads in the hushed silences of high-vaulted cathedrals. I have known most of the leaders in the field of evangelism and have been intimately acquainted with most of the better-known mass evangelists—some of whom are dedicated men and some of whom are rogues.

These facts are mentioned to make it clear that what follows does not grow out of an experience limited to any one denomination, any one approach to theology, or any one country. The views expressed are not academic theories fashioned in isolation from events but have been forged in the heat and pressure of practice.

The contents of this book was given as the James Sprunt Lectures at Union Theological Seminary in Virginia in February of this year. With this book the writer closes a chapter in his life—that of the itinerant evangelist—to give himself to other ministries. It is his hope that the things learned across the past twenty years and here inscribed will contribute to a better understanding of that most frequently misunderstood and most abused aspect of the Church's ministry . . . evangelism.

CHARLES TEMPLETON

New York City
April, 1957

EVANGELISM FOR TOMORROW

THERE IS a fundamental perversity in man that causes his best-laid plans to go awry. We fashion the miracle of flight only to load the wings with destruction. We shrink the world with improved transportation and then make our very proximity our danger. The physicist probes to the heart of the atom only to use the power resident there to reduce his fellows to atoms. Wireless spans the world only to become the instrument of propaganda and the cold war. Give us printing presses with which to put good books within the reach of every man, and we build bigger presses to flood the newsstands with pornography, comic books and Mickey Spillane. Give us television to provide information and recreation, and we crowd the screen with low comedy and bloody it up with crime . . .

I.
Against This Background

THAT THESE are troubled and tumultuous times needs no authentication. Life in the atomic age has been described as "the predicament that precedes death." The world has moved to the edge of an abyss from which there may be no drawing back and stands teetering on the rim. The antipathies between men and nations do not abate, and it would be a bland and facile optimism that would see any certain solution in any near tomorrow.

The exploding of the atomic bomb opened a "Pandora's box" in which—after the first frantic reaction—hope may be discerned at bottom. The Bomb, for all its evil potential, may have acted as a deterrent to global war and is already beginning to yield some of its benefits. Nevertheless, the tensions of the world are no longer mere matters of national rivalry or strategic maneuvers in the game of power politics; they now threaten to burst the world at the seams. Man's "total depravity" has finally devised the means for total destruction. In the face of our dilemma, even the scientists have turned evangelists and are crying, "Except we repent we shall . . . perish!" "What must we do to be saved?" is no longer a merely religious question—survival is at stake.

It seems incredible that events should have come to such a pass when it is remembered with what boundless optimism the twentieth century was greeted. What a trumpeting of hope there was! With what unclouded vision men prophesied of tomorrow! "There is no god but Reason," went the creed, "and Enlightenment is its prophet!" "Glory to man in the highest, for man is the measure of things" was the hymn of praise. A sentence by Robert Louis Stevenson articulated the mood: "The world is so full of a number of things; I'm sure we shall all be as happy as kings."

And there it was in all of its imagined glory—"the world of tomorrow"; the chrome-plated, mass-produced, synthetic and sophisticated "brave new world" of tomorrow! A world in which science reigns supreme, in which war is dead, in which our neuroses and maladjustments have all been resolved by perfected psychiatric techniques; a Utopia from which poverty and ignorance have been banished, where every prospect pleases and where not even man is vile.

But alas!—for all the grandeur of the dream, there was a fatal flaw; the central character in the drama . . . Man!

The dream forgot that the dreamer may also be a destroyer. The Dr. Jekyl who heals the world's ills has an alter ego— and his name is Mr. Hyde!

The dream became a nightmare because it forgot that progress is not measured in bathtubs and Cadillacs or in man's conquest of nature; it is measured in man's conquest of himself. It forgot that none of the things resulting from man's scientific and technological skill are, in themselves, good or evil. Their potential for good and evil is determined by the use to which they are put. We have found that we are wise enough to build the Bomb but not good enough to be trusted with it.

There is a fundamental perversity in man that causes his best-laid plans to go awry. We fashion the miracle of flight only to load the wings with destruction. We shrink the world with improved transportation and then make our very proximity our danger. The physicist probes to the heart of the atom only to use its power to reduce his fellows to atoms. Wireless spans the world only to become the instrument of propaganda and the cold war. The world becomes a neighborhood only to divide into two armed camps from which the nations glower at each other and trigger their earthquakes. Give us printing presses with which to put good books within the reach of every man, and we build bigger presses to flood the newsstands with pornography, comic books and Mickey Spillane. Give us television to provide information and recreation, and we crowd the screen with low comedy and bloody it up with crime. Let our assembly lines pour forth ten thousand creature comforts and we react by developing a vast ennui, an unprecedented number of neuroses and psychosomatic ills, an increasing break- down of the marriage relationship and a terrifying increase in juvenile crime.

We seem to have found all the answers but the important ones: how to live with God, with others and with ourselves. We thought of knowledge as wisdom only to discover that knowledge apart from goodness is dangerous. In the words of Fulton Sheen: "All you do when you educate some men is to turn a stupid devil into a clever devil."—and so make him the more dangerous! Slowly it is beginning to dawn upon us that science cannot in itself become a savior for it is amoral, and unless we match our scientific and techno- logical progress with a corresponding moral progress we will create a Frankenstein's "monster" that will turn on its creator and destroy him. Though still captivated by our material prosperity and by the wonder and authority of science we are becoming increasingly aware that somehow, for all our dreams, we have blundered down a dead-end street. Events have forced us to lift our eyes from the plethora of comforts and conveniences to contemplate that in large measure we are spiritually bankrupt.

Until recently, Americans have always had a vast self- confidence. They have come by it legitimately, for Ameri- cans have performed one of the most prodigious feats in history; in less than one hundred and fifty years they have transformed a wilderness into the richest and strongest nation of all time. Nothing seemed impossible. A visiting preacher from Scotland said recently, after a tour of the nation, "I don't know how I would preach to this people. I would be afraid to say to Americans, 'You can't save yourself,' for fear someone would stand up, spit on his hands, and say, 'Oh, *can't* I?' "

But a change has come. For the first time in their history Americans are doubting themselves and the future. The advent of the atomic age, the enormity of world problems, the impersonality of government and the apparent unimportance of the individual in a mass society all conspire to vitiate optimism and point up the baffling complexity of our age. It was said after the Korean War that "America has at last learned that the 'happy ending' is a myth." Arthur Miller in his play, *Death of a Salesman,* has written a description of millions of Americans in his epitaph for Willie Loman: "Poor guy . . . he didn't know who he was."

It is to this nation—a nation in mid-stream—that the Christian Church must address itself. What a staggering challenge! What a task even to understand America—complex contradictory colossus that she is; seething, yeasting, vital organism that she is!

> . . . half-brother of the world.
> With something good and bad of every land.

The man who would hope by "the foolishness of preaching" to challenge the attention of this astonishing nation and call her to response must needs be either a consummate egotist or a man of faith!

For America is the great paradox. She is tough-minded and materialistic and at the same time the author of the Marshall Plan—an act of benevolence described as "the greatest single act of altruism in the history of nations." She is certain success is measured in the accumulation of "things" and at the same time is crowding her churches as never before. Somehow she manages to worship *both* Almighty God and the almighty dollar. She is religiously illiterate—subsisting second hand on a Christian heritage, and torn between the persistent memory of yesterday's mores and today's unconventionality. She has a distaste for discipline and a suspicion of governmental interference in civil affairs but continues to move toward an increasing regimentation of her life and a growing bureaucracy.

America's paradoxical nature may clearly be seen in her attitude toward religious faith. Americans are religious: a nation-wide poll revealed that some 96 per cent believe in God (the vast majority subscribing to a trinitarian concept and stating that prayer, heaven, hell, et cetera are facts to which they give mental assent). Americans are religious: approximately one hundred million belong to the churches. Americans are religious: the membership of the Church grows faster proportionately than the population, with more people attending church than at any previous period in history. Americans are religious: there has not been a week in the past decade when the literary "best seller" listings have not included at least one religious title. The Bible continues easily to outsell all other books. Motion pictures with religious themes are outstanding box-office draws. Mass evangelists speak to crowds numbering in the tens of thousands. Every major political speech ends on a religious note. The Pledge of Allegiance has been altered by act of Congress to read, ". . . this nation *under* God."

However, concern is not commitment. A revival of interest in religion is not a revival of religion. Professor A. Roy Eckhardt of Lehigh University, commenting on the current resurgence of religious interest, said: "Piety is more and more diffusing itself among our people, particularly in ways that supplement the regular ministry of the churches. It hardly follows that the new piety is to be accepted uncritically. There is nothing in the Bible to support the view that religion is necessarily a good thing. On the contrary, the Bible is suspicious of much that passes for religion."

How to account for the increased interest? A large number of clergymen in many sections of the country listed the following reasons:

The sense of insecurity growing out of the advent of the atomic age and the continuing world crisis.

The emergence of such popular religious leaders as Fulton Sheen, Billy Graham and Norman Vincent Peale.

The rediscovery of the layman as the Church's Evangelist.

The publicity related to the incidence of juvenile delinquency and the consequent concern of parents for the moral training of their children.

Improved means for proclaiming the gospel.

Social approval of churchgoing.

The establishment of effective departments of evangelism by the major denominations.

The increased attractiveness of religious literature.

A general improvement in preaching.

The participation of national leaders (from the President on down) in religious activity.

The need for social contacts in an increasingly mobile nation.

The war experiences of men in the armed services.

The "easy membership" of many churches.

The boom in the construction of new and attractive church buildings.

Many other reasons (including the operation of the sovereign purpose of God) were also suggested—it being recognized, however, that while they may have contributed to the return of religion, some were unwholesome.

We would err in assuming that the nation's increased religiosity means that Americans are becoming more religious. The gratification commonly expressed by churchmen at the statistical gains of recent years must be tempered by other facts. The very acceptance of the Church reflected in the statistics is an evidence of weakness, for the added numerical strength is not visible in a growing moral power. Statistical columns reveal a nation increasingly Christian; the news columns reveal a mounting paganism. Coincident with the increase in Church membership is an increase in lawlessness and crime. These apparently encouraging statistics provide cold comfort, for while it is true that there are over one hundred million Americans on the rolls of the churches and synagogues, it is also true that on any given Sunday not more than two fifths of that membership is in attendance. All of which means that on the average Sunday somewhere between eighty and one hundred million Americans do not trouble themselves corporately to worship God. Beyond this there is the fact that much of the active membership of the Church is indistinguishable from those on the outside.

While the impress of religion on American life is broad, it is shallow. The relevance of faith to specific life situations is not always clear. A man's religion tends to be isolated from his daily responsibilities; it does not move easily from pew to market place. While there is little intellectual atheism, there is often a formless skepticism concerning the supernatural aspects of religion. The Church is a cherished institution but (while there are, of course, notable exceptions) it wields little direct influence upon the thinking of millions within its membership. All too frequently Christians who readily admit the existence of God deny His Lordship in practice. "Much of the atheism of our time is unconscious, unargued and implicit."

The average church member has little grasp of the meaning of the faith he espouses. Though natively religious, Americans are religiously illiterate. Many a church member matures in every area of life except the religious, continuing to hold to concepts about the nature and will of God learned in childhood. A Presbyterian, say, might be unable to state succinctly why he is a Presbyterian rather than a Methodist or a Baptist. He might have difficulty explaining just what he means on Sunday morning when he says, "I believe in . . . the Holy Catholic Church, the communion of saints, the forgiveness of sins, and the life everlasting. . . ."

Before we analyze the great changes in the environment and attitudes of the contemporary American it is necessary to temper the rather negative appraisal given above by a recognition of the many signs of religious and moral health in the nation. Not infrequently, preachers in speaking of the contemporary predicament, overstate man's disorder in the interests of a kind of evangelistic polemic and paint an inaccurate and forbidding picture, quite unrecognizable to the listener.

The headlines, making much of delinquency among juveniles, overlook the fact that there are currently more candidates for the Christian ministry than at any time in American history, and a host of young people maintaining high moral standards in an age dominated by materialism and sensuality. The Johnny Rays and the Elvis Presleys are, in their appeal, balanced by the enormous sale of classical recorded music and hi-fi playback equipment. Highly publicized violations of public or private trust are more than balanced by the scrupulously honest business and professional dealings of thousands of businessmen. The "conspiracy of mediocrity" often fomented by the media of mass entertainment is compensated for, in part, by the millions of men and women of all ages involved in serious scholarship and intellectual pursuit. The undisciplined gratification of the senses must have held over against it the enormous volume of altruistic and philanthropic activity in which millions of Americans are engaged. Life in the United States is undoubtedly at a point of crisis, but it is not devoid of heartening aspects. This must be borne in mind by the observer who might tend too readily to "view with alarm."

Let us turn now from the general background against which the Church labors, to the individual American who must be confronted. It must first be said of him that he is blood brother of every other man in history. While his civilization is bigger, faster, more complex and more complicated than that of previous centuries, his basic nature and his basic problems remain the same. Written over history are the words, "Everything changes; nothing changes." The fleshpots of Egypt, the couches and flagons of Rome, the riot and revelry of the Dark Ages, and the fast-moving, fast-drinking, cushioned and upholstered age in which he lives are all cut from the same cloth. "Change and decay in all around I see," said the hymn writer in the nineteenth century; he could just as well have said it in the first.

This identity with his predecessors having been asserted, the Church—if it would hope to speak to him with insight— must also recognize that the contemporary American's life is in many ways unique. Changes in the world and in the fabric of society in recent decades place this generation in a radically different situation from its forebears. For all of our basic similarities, we are different from our predecessors: different in the things we do, in the things we talk about, in the things we read, in the amusements we enjoy, in the mobility of our life, and in our relationships to one another and to the rest of the world.

We are different in relation to our *homes*. This is a generation on the move. One out of every six Americans moves his place of residence on an average of every ten years. A nation cannot encompass this kind of mobility without having its way of life profoundly affected. The familiar patterns of neighborhood and school and work get broken. Many people become rootless. The old picture of the family homestead dims. The artisan handing down his inherited craft to his children becomes a rarity.

We are different in relation to our *work*. Work has come to assume a more important place in our lives. It has given to women, especially, a new status in society and has profoundly affected the concept of home and parenthood. Work and not neighborhood now brings about our main contacts with other people. Automation and the assembly line have changed the character of much of the work that is done, many men and women becoming little more than extensions of the machine. It must be realized that this lack of personal, creative involvement in work engenders problems, for if life is meaningless at work it is difficult to find meaning elsewhere.

We are different in relation to our *amusements*. We have

become victims of "spectatoritis"—nonparticipation in our amusements except through identification with the performers. The television screen in the home, the cinemascope screen in the theater, the enormous sport spectacles and the easy "reading" of picture magazines and comic books provide the entertainment for the majority of the nation. For every active participant there are a thousand spectators. We take for granted the universality and uniformity of amusement today and fail to realize that it is something new. And it is not without very real advantages, for great music, great drama and sheer "escape entertainment" are now within the reach of millions where they were once the regular privilege of the few. For the first time in history a uniform background for a nation's leisure life has been erected and its influence upon the future will be profound.

We are different in our relation to *education*. We are sometimes shocked at what people read, forgetting to be surprised that they read at all! It has not always been so. The cigar-store Indian, the barber pole and the apothecary jar are reminders of a day not long gone when a largely illiterate population recognized places of business by visual representations rather than by words. Today in the United States illiteracy is the exception rather than the rule. A great proportion of the population is high school and college trained. Moreover, the scope of the average American's interest has been extended by the radio, television and the printing press. He knows something of what is happening in the world in a way his grandfather did not. He knows that what happens in China, Russia and Africa profoundly affects his own way of life. He or one of his immediate family has probably been abroad—in war, on a vacation or on business. His opinions about the world may be ill-formed and uninformed but he is aware that there are other ways of life and other faiths in the world and it has influenced his outlook and will influence his judgments.

The American mind to which the Church must address itself is a complex structure. It is all cluttered up with snippets and patches of information, a veritable hodgepodge of bits of half-understood science, magazine morality, pseudo-Christianity and humanistic idealism. Americans are enchanted by the glamor of a "success culture" but are haunted by the memory of their puritanical antecedents. Daily we are brainwashed with ideas born on Broadway at 42nd Street and Hollywood at Vine. Raised in a climate of freedom of speech, we are given to self-expression but seldom stop to inquire whether we have a self worthy to be expressed.

We fear old age and struggle desperately to remain young (to the point where maturity, aping youth and afraid to smile lest it betray a wrinkle, is a commonplace). We fear death and use cosmetics to make our dead look as though they are in the bloom of health. We worship youth, beauty, wealth, success, athletic proficiency and the female bosom. We want religious faith without discipline, world peace without world involvement, and increased social security with lowered taxes. We unconsciously resent having been thrust into the position of having to provide world leadership and tend to labor under the impression that dollars and the imposition of our way of life will automatically resolve international problems. We are a young nation with young traditions and have grown confused with the complexity of the problems related to our economy, our racial tensions, our changing culture, and our world responsibility. It is likely that no other young nation in history has ever had to face such a diversity of complicated internal and external dilemmas.

To help fix the troubled, perplexed mind of the contemporary American on Him "Whom to know is life eternal" is the infinitely difficult task of the Church. The problem is complicated by the fact that America is a nominally Christian nation which, while not opposed to the Christian message as invalid, is unmoved by it and likely to ignore it as unimportant. Moreover, the serious divisions of the Church militate against a concerted witness and make unlikely any large-scale co-ordinated thrust in our generation.

WE HAVE grown soft in prosperity. Our membership rolls are fat, our buildings are luxurious, our endowments seem to secure the future, our faith finds general approval. One would not disparage achievement or betray a guilt complex by lusting after persecution, but there is the danger that the Church will not so much convert the world as be converted by the world to its way of life. Living too close to society and not daring to condemn with too great vigor the sins to which it is itself given, the Church stands in danger that the time will come when (to paraphrase G. K. Chesterton) it can pick up a microphone and address the entire world—only to find it has nothing to say.

II.
The Contemporary Opportunity

CONFRONTED WITH the enormous challenge to evangelize the world at mid-century, the Christian Church is not responding with the forthrightness, dedication and power that is needed. Too often it is occupied in fighting a defensive action. Too frequently it has seemed uncertain.

In recent decades the Church has suffered four major onslaughts: an attack on the Bible, bringing grave doubts to millions as to its inspiration and authority; an assault by atheistic communism, nullifying many of the great gains of the modern missionary movement; the impact of the authority of the material sciences—the achievements and conclusions often seeming to conflict with and overshadow religious truth; and the emergence of the new science of psychiatry, apparently outmoding Christian concepts of man's nature and moral responsibility.

To such attacks, Christians reacted in a number of ways. Some fell into a mood of accommodation and lost the vitality of faith needed to shape and give direction to a generation trying to orient itself; some, by retreating into a static orthodoxy and a stubborn biblicism, lost claim to influence among thoughtful people; others, examining their faith in the light of a maturing Christian theology, have discovered new resources with which to strengthen their own lives and effectively confront their time.

One thing is clear: If the Church is going to make an impress upon society it is going to have to *be* the Church. It cannot hope to rediscover its own genius or lay claim to the serious attention of its contemporaries if it offers anything but an authentic word from God. It must repent of its own sins of division, complacency, spiritual pride and partial commitment before it dares to call others to commitment. Emil Brunner has said, "The greatest sin of the Church is that she withholds the gospel from herself and from the world." The Church must bring its own life under the judgment of the gospel before it can hope to herald its message with conviction and effectiveness.

The Church must recognize and repudiate the contemporary substitutes for the gospel to which it has so often given emphasis: that equating of respectability with Christianity which seeks only creedal conformity—as though the proof of piety is dignified sobriety; that shallow evangelism which is interested only in getting "decisions for Christ" and is unconcerned about Christian nurture and social responsibility; that offering of a palliative rather than a cross on the assumption that the goal of the Christian life is peace of mind; that so-called "spiritual" gospel which gives the impression that man is soul and body and that the Church is interested only in the soul; that obscurantism which confuses faith with gullibility and refuses to love God with the whole mind; that substitution of technique for compassion which treats persons as things and manipulates human personality to serve egotistical ends; and that "hellenizing" of the gospel—attempting to communicate it by logic rather than by proclamation.

At best, nothing in all the world can stand in the same company with the Church. But too often the Church has not been at its best. Too often it has given the impression that it is designed to preserve the status quo; that its principal mission is to create patience and resignation, to bury the dead, to talk in an unnatural way about the world to come, and to say too little of relevance about the world in which we live. Too often the Church has lost its stringent note in its eagerness to appease the State and the world. Sometimes it has even permitted evils to flourish in its shadow. As a consequence, the man in the street has looked on and has seen no reason to be challenged.

A striking Old Testament phrase describes the Church as " terrible as an army with banners." But is it? Surely one would not for a moment forget that the Church has always had its heroes and those who have been in the van in every great issue, but too often the majority, on whom attendance upon divine worship acts primarily as a soporific, have created the impression that the Church is not so much an armory as an infirmary.

It is the duty of the Church to maintain the reality of KOINONIA—that unique Christian fellowship with its vertical and horizontal aspects. It is the calling of the Church to herald "the good news"—to speak without equivocation and in love the throbbing reality of God's redemptive overture in Jesus Christ. It is the responsibility of the Church to bring the gospel to bear upon society— to relate the love of God to every human situation. But "where the trumpet is expected the flute will not suffice." The Church cannot merely whisper its protest against social evils so flagrant that they seem to take tongue and proclaim their injustice. KOINONIA is impossible in a congregation so low in its standards that, as has been quipped, it will enroll as a "believer" anyone who has been heard to say, "Thank God, it's quit raining." The world will not be brought up short by such sermon themes as "Paddling with John Around Patmos."

Karl Barth, in a speech read over the British Broadcasting Corporation a few years ago, said that if he were a politician or an editor of a newspaper he would ask the churches of the land the following questions:

Why are you not saying what you ought to say, and saying it with power and eloquence? Why don't you force us to pay attention to you and listen to you? We should like to see you less timid, more consistent, bolder. We often have the impression that you are afraid—of what, really? And you spread so little light and joy around you. When you make yourselves heard, it is usually with cares and complaints, lamentations and accusations.

We are too timid. Too frequently we comport ourselves like sycophants, seeking to please and to mollify. We convey the impression that persons of note in a community are conferring a favor upon God and the Church by attending the worship service or by joining the membership. This obsequiousness is in part the consequence of our magnifying the priestly ministry and minimizing the prophetic. The priest is seldom persecuted, for he stands *with the people* pleading with God; the prophet is frequently persecuted because he stands *with God* echoing His demands and speaking His commandments.

The minister who would be true to his calling will be both priest and prophet—standing with the people and with God. He will know that while he has been called to be "the servant of all," he is not called to be a lackey. He is no salesman seeking the approval of a prospective customer; he is a spokesman for the Almighty and must needs sometimes run counter to the standards by which men live. He dare not seek the universal approval of the community lest he fall under the pronouncement, "Woe unto you when all men speak well of you." An ancient Eastern writer has put it this way:

If I shoved a plow, if I kept a flock, if I cultivated a garden, if I mended old clothes, none would notice me, few would consider me, not many would find fault with me and I could easily please everybody. But, for having been studious of the field of nature, solicitous for the pasture of the soul, enamored of the cultivation of the mind—a very Daedalus fashioning raiment for the intellect—every passer-by threatens me, everyone who sees me attacks me, who comes upon me rends me, who lays hold on me devours. It is not one, it is not few; it is many, it is almost all. If you would know why this is, I will tell you the reason of it . . . *I am a warner!*

We have grown soft in prosperity. Our membership rolls are fat, our buildings are luxurious, our endowments seem to secure the future, our faith finds general approval. One would not disparage achievement or betray a guilt complex by lusting after persecution, but there is the danger that the Church will not so much convert the world as be converted by the world to *its* way of life. Ease is not good for those who have "no continuing city." There are sections in the gospel that sound a little incongruous when spoken in a church luxuriating in "an abundance of things." Living too close to society, and not daring to condemn with too great vigor the sins to which it is itself given, the Church stands in danger that the time will come when (to paraphrase G. K. Chesterton) it can pick up a microphone and address the entire world—only to find it has nothing to say.

"Let the Church be the Church," said the Ecumenical Congress at Oxford. Let it no longer withhold the gospel from itself and from the world. Let it bring its own life under judgment, and in repentance and renewed commitment carry the good news to the nation and the world. For, with all its failings, the Church has great virtues and tremendous vitality. In the words of Newton: "If the Ark of the Lord seems to be slipping, it is not so; it is due merely to a swimming in your own head."

Our resources are many: the presence of the Spirit of Christ as the living Lord of the Church, a hard core of dedicated men and women whose hearts and hands and minds have been given to the Christian cause, an expanding theology informing the proclamation of the gospel and guarding the Church from heresy, an enormous good will born of ten thousand philanthropies, a network of outposts unequaled by any organization in the world, a literate and often deeply committed ministry, a growing group of dedicated laymen, an ever-improving teaching apparatus, a record of opposition to tyranny, and the realization that —in the words of Reinhold Niebuhr—"nothing short of the knowledge of the true God will save [men] from the impiety of making themselves God and the cruelty of seeing their fellow men as devils because they are involved in the same pretension."

The Church seems to be facing the greatest opportunity in its long history: the current widespread hunger for spiritual certainty. Christians believe that the anxiety, fear, and frustration of our day are only further evidences of the timeless longing of men for God and that these and other needs find their resolution in the response to the Christian gospel.

Aware of laying itself open to the charge of naïve over-simplification, and conscious of the danger resident in glib and facile slogans, the Church cries with ever-deepening conviction, "Christ is the answer!" The Samaritan woman, speaking of Jesus, gave the Church its statement of faith (Phillips' translation): "We are convinced that this is the man who will save the world." Two thousand years ago the world turned a corner and came upon Jesus Christ. *He* is the message of the Church; not his teaching or his example alone, but he, himself. Whatever else the Church may have to apologize for, it need never apologize for *him!*

For all the difficulties in its path, the Church has possibly never had a greater opportunity since the period of its birth. The early Christians sat at the deathbed of an age. Greece and Rome, the dominant forces of their time, were about to pass from the scene and a new era was about to be born. Now we too sit at the deathbed of an age. There have been more changes in the past fifty years than in the previous two thousand. Just as Rome prepared the then-known world for the spreading of the gospel, commerce has done in our time. Once again a *lingua franca* (in this instance, English) enables us to sound the message in every part of the globe. The task looks forbidding to any but men of faith. It is not irresponsible optimism to say "With God, all things are possible"—it is a Christian rallying cry which has been vindicated again and again in history. Is the present task any more difficult than that facing the little band of a dozen wanderers centuries ago? Who would have thought to describe the pagan Roman world as "a field white already to harvest"?

This is one of those times in history when "one can hear the kingdom of God thundering at the gates." In the words of a great Christian statesman, "These are times when the soul of humanity is being plowed up and being made ready for the planting of the seed." Does it sound like naïve optimism to cry, "Evangelize the world in our generation"? We can deny the possibility no longer, for it has been done —the Communists have done it! In a single generation they have carried their ideas to every nation on earth and infiltrated every level of society. The Communist is the greatest "evangelist" to appear since the Early Church "went everywhere" preaching the gospel. He is sweeping the world off its feet with a passion that makes ours look pale by comparison, and if we are to meet his challenge (only part of our task, for the Church must never think of the gospel as a mere antidote to communism and must remember that the task is not to hate Communists but to be the instrument of their conversion) we must have something of the dedication that sped the early Church to its mission and made its witness effectual.

How may the contemporary church respond to its challenge? It may take one of three attitudes: It may retreat into a parochial isolationism as did the priests who said to Judas in his remorse, "What is that to us? See *thou* to that"; or, staggered by the enormity of the challenge, it may echo the words of Hamlet, "The time is out of joint," or it may respond as did Rupert Brooke in another troubled time, "Now God be thanked Who matched us with this hour!"

Let what has been said be summed up in the words of Karl Barth:

The world which we confront today is aggressively pagan. Many influences and agencies in modern life work to undermine the Christian view of life, and subtly to convert even Church people from an outright Christian faith. The only adequate answer is for Christians to recover the New Testament power of spiritual aggression. That demands an ability to witness convincingly and positively on behalf of our faith. It is not sufficient for Christians to content themselves with being Disciples (learners) of Jesus Christ. Our calling is to be Apostles (messengers) of Jesus Christ to every man and in every realm of life.

THE CHURCH must not only return to evangelism, it must rethink it. Evangelistic activity is not an unmixed blessing. Fundamental as it is to the work of the Church, evangelism is peculiarly subject to abuses and excess and, unless the Church beware, may become a threat to its unity and to a maturing Christian faith. The proper expression of evangelism will add numbers and vitality to the Church, but bad evangelism can have a fragmenting and baneful influence. As with atomic power, evangelism may be a creative or a destructive force.

III.
Toward a Concept
of Evangelism

No PART of the work of the Church is so subject to confused thinking and excess as is evangelism. It has been said that "where you have two Christians you have three opinions," and this diversity is nowhere more evident than in the matter of evangelism.

There are always some in the Church who are enthusiastically *for* evangelism and look with no little suspicion upon those who do not share their view. There are always some who are *against* evangelism for what they consider good and sufficient reasons and who regard the first group as naïve and overzealous. The majority tend to be like the man who was asked if he believed in God. He replied, "Well, there are some who say there is a God and

31

some who say there is not; as for me, I stand somewhere between these two extremes."

Unfortunately, some much given to the practice of evangelism have brought more zeal than wisdom to the task. Others have often taken a purely negative attitude, acutely aware of the dangers and improprieties into which evangelism can fall and quite vocal about the kind of evangelism they *don't* believe in, but not nearly so articulate as to the kind they *do*.

Apart from these extremes, however, many thoughtful Christians hold serious doubts as to the validity and permanent effectiveness of any attempt to bring about Christian commitment in others. They are convinced that

> There is no expeditious road
> To pack and label souls for God
> And win them by the barrel-load.

Their doubt as to the legitimacy and the effectiveness of evangelism is matched by an antipathy to the methods employed by some evangelists. Many people have only the most unsavory memories of evangelistic services. They equate evangelism with revivalism and, in rejecting revivalism, reject evangelism through prejudice.

Later in this section we shall come to a statement about the nature of evangelism, but let us first indicate some of the ways by which the Church has confounded the methods by which evangelism has been done with evangelism itself.

Evangelism has been confused with *revivalism*—the pattern which evangelism took in the nineteenth century and subsequently.

Evangelism has been identified with *religious education*—the carrying of Horace Bushnell's *"Christian nurture"* concept to an extreme.

Evangelism has been identified with *emotionalism*—the frenetic and sometimes weird activity of the snake-handlers, the so-called "holy rollers" and others.

Evangelism has been equated with *"soul-saving"*—the over-concern with the salvation of the individual with little sensitivity to the relation of the gospel to social responsibility.

Evangelism has been identified with *lay visitation*—the revival of the New Testament two-by-two home visitation by laymen.

The Church is just emerging from a retreat from evangelism that started, roughly, with the ending of World War I. The withdrawal began with a vague uneasiness about the evangelism then current, was accelerated by a number of coincident circumstances, and finally plunged the Church into an exaggerated reaction from which it has only recently begun to recover.

The period of decline in evangelism was one of theological optimism, a time when a self-consciously rational Church began not only to distrust but actually to deny many of the premises from which evangelism proceeds. The historical method of criticism as applied to the Bible, while it provided a better understanding of the Bible and a faith more firmly rooted in history, disturbed the beliefs of many Christians as to the ground of their faith. Many critics went to extremes—some denying every supernatural element in the record and even the historic existence of such a person as Jesus of Nazareth—and while many of the extremes were not the conclusions of the most reputable critics and did not find wide acceptance among the best Christian scholars, they did influence the thinking of great numbers and added to the growing skepticism about the reliability of the Bible as a historical record and its validity as revelation. Subsequently, as the central affirmations of traditional Christian faith were in process of being rethought and restated, the sense of urgency diminished.

During the period of decline in evangelism the relatively new science of psychology was gaining widespread acceptance. The conviction emerged that the common patterns of evangelism might be injurious to mental health and that the spiritual phenomena associated in the past with Christian experience could be accounted for in terms of normal and abnormal psychology.

Further, it was a period of growing interest in Christian education. In a Church reacting to a static orthodoxy and sometimes tending toward "liberalism," this frequently led to the substitution of education as a natural and healthy alternative to revivalism.

In addition, the "roaring twenties," with its disdain for discipline and its unflagging quest for pleasure, provided a climate anything but conducive to the kind of evangelism then in vogue.

However, the principal reason for the repudiation of evangelism was, perhaps, the excesses committed by evangelists. Careless thinking tended to confuse evangelism with revivalism, and the irresponsible crudities and excesses of many of the mass evangelists of that era provoked strong reaction to evangelism as such. Not infrequently the revivalists' appeals for decision were almost entirely emotional and the aftermath disillusioning and dangerous to mental health. Converts were often led into an unbalanced approach to Christian living without any understanding of the importance of worship and service. Too often the follow-up was pitifully inadequate. Too often the evangelist attacked the organized Church and became the instrument of division. Too often the dollar sign was more evident than the sign of the cross as the evangelist found it difficult not to love that "love-offering." Too often the evangelist was a strongly opinionated individualist, given to sensationalism and with no sense of identification with and responsibility to the Church. Too often the theological content of his appeals was negligible and the emphasis predominantly negative.

These are some of the reasons why a strong reaction to evangelism took place within the Church and why in the twenty-five years following World War I the very term "evangelism" was suspect in what has been described as the "standard-brand" churches.

It is, however, a pity that in reaction to an unbalanced and unchristian approach to evangelism many churches have lost the evangelistic note from their ministry. A church that fails to evangelize has within it the seeds of death and cannot long remain a vital organism. When the sense of urgency and the recognition of the centrality of evangelism is lost, Christianity tends to become an ethic rather vaguely connected with an ancient, supernaturalistic religion, with little relevance to daily life. Christianity becomes mere respectability (one is a Christian because he belongs to a church, refrains from the more flagrant wrongs, and believes in God) and seemliness and dignity become the distinguishing marks of the Church at worship.

Happily the tide is turning. The Church's evangelistic concern, having ebbed for a generation, is again coming to the flood. Evangelism is returning to the heart of the Church and, while many remain doubtful as to its eventual effect, the temper of our times and the dilemma of the Church is forcing a reconsideration of the nature of evangelism and its place in the Church. It is becoming clear that no placid, innocuous moralism, no mere subscription to a magnificent idealism can challenge the enormous paganism of our time, and thoughtful churchmen are again examining the content and manner of the Church's witness.

But the Church must not only return to evangelism, it must rethink it. Evangelistic activity is not an unmixed blessing. Fundamental as it is to the work of the Church, evangelism is peculiarly subject to abuses and excess and, unless the Church beware, may become a threat to its unity and to a maturing Christian faith. The proper expression of evangelism will add numbers and vitality to the Church, but bad evangelism can have a fragmenting and baneful influence. As with atomic power, evangelism may be a creative or a destructive force.

The Church must rethink evangelism. It would be a grave mistake merely to unearth the terms and techniques of the evangelism of the past. Care must be taken not to fall again into the errors which, in the past, made it properly suspect. George Sweazey has said, "Evangelism is always dangerous —though not so dangerous as the lack of evangelism." The Church must come to an adequate concept of evangelism and no longer identify it with particular activities traditionally associated with it. The Church must realize that the proclamation of the evangel is not a spasmodic activity and the special province of a few, but the responsibility of *all* Christians at *all* times. A "theology of evangelism" must emerge that will hold in balance the flaming heart and the disciplined mind.

Evangelism is one of the great terms in the Christian heritage, its root going back to the origins of Christianity, to the "good news"—the evangel—which Jesus came to proclaim. The prologue to John's gospel outlines the genesis of evangelism. If one asks *"Who* is the evangelist?" one is confronted immediately with the diverse meanings the term has come to convey. In the ultimate sense, God the Father is the Evangelist, initiating the appeal to the will of man and, by His Spirit, making His appeal through us. Jesus is the Evangelist who comes proclaiming the good news and urging men to believe it. Clement of Alexandria and others in the early Church sometimes held that the eternal Word is the Evangelist, bidding all men in every age to forsake falsehood and embrace the truth.

There are three New Testament references to evangelists. In Ephesians 4 they appear as a group ordained by Christ within the Church, in Acts 21 Phillip is spoken of as an "evangelist," and in II Timothy 4 Timothy is enjoined by Paul to "do the work of an evangelist."

The burden of New Testament emphasis would seem to indicate that the Church is the evangelist and that although the evangelistic task is the responsibility of every Christian it is laid in a special way upon certain Christians. There is evidence that the term "evangelist" was used to designate not only a preacher of the gospel but one who had a particular kind of work to do. The term "evangelist" denoted a *function* rather than an *office* and there was no exclusive class of evangelists. Men became evangelists not so much because they were specifically set apart for evangelistic work, but because they entered upon it through extraordinary qualifications or felt called to it. They tended to be itinerant and were usually the first to bring the gospel to a community. This is not to suggest that others in the Church did not engage in evangelistic work; the Apostles were evangelists as were, at times, the pastors and teachers.

The term "evangelist," interestingly enough, does not appear in the writings of the apostolic fathers or in the Didache. It seems reasonable to assume that, inasmuch as one of their principal responsibilities was teaching, evangelists came to be included in the general class called "teachers." Whatever the reason, the title disappeared in its original signification and came to be applied exclusively to the writers of the four Gospels. Matthew, Mark, Luke, and John were known as "the Evangelists," as they are still called today.

It was not until the time of the Reformation that the term and its derivatives again appeared in common use. The term "evangelical" came to be applied to certain groups within the Church (in particular those associated with the Reformation) because of their emphasis on the preaching of the gospel of grace in contrast to the legalistic tendency of Roman Catholic teaching. Gradually "evangelical" became descriptive of both the Lutheran and Reformed Churches to denote a difference of emphasis on the gospel of grace as distinguished from religious legalism and sacramentalism. In parts of Europe it came to mean simply anticatholic and even antireligious.

In the eighteenth century "evangelical" designated a branch of the Church of England—later known as the Low Church—by way of distinguishing it from the High and Broad Church. This low or "evangelical" wing of the Church of England represented the same doctrinal emphasis and the same evangelistic fervor that informed the Methodist revival, with which the Low Church was in general sympathy. That the Low Church group was not too highly regarded by those who differed with them is indicated by a comment by Mr. Sidney Smith in 1808:

We shall use the general term "evangelical" to designate those three classes of fanatics (Arminian and Calvinistic Methodists and the Evangelical clergy of the Church of England), not troubling ourselves to point out the finer shades and nicer discriminations of lunacy, but treating them all as in one general conspiracy against common sense and rational orthodoxy.

Over the years a distinction in usage arose between the words "evangelical" and "evangelistic." By derivation they would seem to be synonymous, but "evangelical" has come to have a broader meaning than "evangelistic." A man might be evangelical without being evangelistic, although it is difficult to conceive of a man being evangelistic without being evangelical. Evangelicalism has come to denote a certain approach to doctrine, whereas evangelism has come to mean the method by which the evangelical faith is propagated. We have come to speak of the "evangelical faith" and the "evangelistic method," the first connoting theology and the second, method.

It is important to arrive at an adequate definition of evangelism, not only because evangelism is a word so frequently misunderstood, but because it is one of the two principal responsibilities of the Church. The Church is called to worship and to witness. Its witness may be made corporately as well as through its individual members, being expressed by the life of the Church in the world as well as in the speech of its clergy and its laity.

There is constant danger that the term "evangelism" will be limited to specific activities related to special preaching efforts and thus become too narrow. The opposite danger is that the term may be used so indiscriminately that it will lose its sense of urgency. In essence, the word evangelism means "outreach." It is the Church extending her arms to encompass with her message and her concern the non-Christians beyond her borders. It is the Church saying in a variety of ways, "We have found something of infinite value (our faith in God); come and share it with us."

Research has unearthed more than fifty specific definitions of evangelism. Many of them are too brief to be comprehensive; others are too lengthy to be useful. The Archbishop's Committee of the Church of England framed a definition of evangelism which later became a part of the "Report of the Archbishop's Commission" (popularly known as "Towards the Conversion of England") and has, with some minor changes, been adopted as a definition of evangelism by the Madras Foreign Missions Council, the National Council of the Churches of Christ in the U. S. A., the Commission on Evangelism of the Presbyterian Church, U. S. A., and other bodies. Its gist is as follows:

Evangelism is so to present Jesus Christ in the power of the Holy Spirit that men shall come to put their trust in God through him, to accept him as their Savior from the guilt and power of sin, to serve him as Lord in the fellowship of the Church and to follow him in the vocations of the common life.

It is evident that this is an excellent statement for it speaks

not only of the proclamation of Christ as Savior, but of
the Christian life.

Let us, however, suggest another definition in the hope
that it will enable us more adequately to present a concept
of evangelism encompassing aspects of the evangelistic task
of the Church commonly neglected or misunderstood.

What is Evangelism? Essentially, evangelism is "the proclamation of the evangel"—the bearing of a witness in any
way and by any means to the good news that "God was in
Christ reconciling the world to Himself." Consequently,
*anything the Church may do which has as its ultimate end
the winning of men and women to Christ and the winning
of Christians to deepened commitment is evangelism.* It is
a bearing witness to the fact that God is not a dispassionate
Deity, isolated from mundane life, but a "Father in Heaven"
whose nature is love and Who has entered into history in
Jesus Christ to effect a reconciliation between man with
Himself, and man with man.

Evangelism has nothing to do, essentially, with *numbers;*
Jesus was an evangelist speaking to the more than five
thousand on a grassy hillside, but he was as much an evangelist seated on a well curb speaking to an individual
Samaritan woman. Evangelism has nothing essentially to
do with *results;* it is estimated that the famed American
evangelist, Billy Sunday, was instrumental in bringing about
more than a million "decisions for Christ" during his life-
time, whereas William Carey, the well-known Baptist missionary, labored ten years in India without seeing a single

convert. Was Carey less an evangelist than Sunday? Evangelism has nothing essentially to do with *methods;* evangelism may be done by a "sawdust trail" revivalist in a tent, by a drum-beating Salvation Army officer on a street corner, by a robed and hooded high-churchman in a great cathedral, by a layman in home visitation, by a teacher in a classroom, by a chaplain in the field, and by a minister in his counseling chamber. It may be done by the printed page and through radio, television and motion pictures. It has nothing essentially to do with specific methods.

The Church at worship bears its witness to the reality of Christian faith. The efforts of the Church in such directions as the attempt to end racial segregation, to get better housing, to feed the hungry, to effect the healing of sick minds and bodies, to halt injustice and to work for peace—all these efforts and others are, as will be shown, evangelism, and bear powerful witness to the reality of the Christian gospel.

Beyond this there is the fact that the Church is not only the evangelizing community, it is, itself, being evangelized through worship and instruction. Evangelism not only has to do with the initial experience by which one enters the Christian Church, but is (through the teaching-ministry) also related to the calling of members of the Church to the commitment of areas of their lives yet unevangelized.

It is unfortunate that there is a tendency in the Church to compartmentalize certain emphases. It is only natural that a man with a sense of vocation in a particular area of the

Church's worship and witness will turn into a specialist. This is unavoidable; carried to extremes it becomes dangerous. All have known the zealous "soul-winner" with little time for liturgical worship, and the earnest liturgist little concerned to win souls. What might be called the catholic tradition in Christendom has always insisted on the primacy of worship; the evangelical tradition has, similarly, insisted on the primacy of evangelism. The New Testament makes it clear that both extremes are wrong; in its pages we see their mutual and inseparable relationship.

Evangelism must be rooted in worship even as worship must lead to some kind of evangelistic activity. No matter how steeped in tradition the liturgy, no matter how aesthetically satisfying the appointments of the sanctuary and the components of the order of worship, no matter how ecstatic the rapture, that worship which does not lead to evangelism is spurious and non-Christian. How can we love God (with that love which worship reveals) if we do not love our neighbor and, in consequence, seek his good out of our concern for his spiritual and material welfare? The first great evangelistic movement was born of the Church's worship. In Acts 13 it is stated that "While they were worshipping the Lord and fasting, the Holy Spirit said, 'Set apart for me, Barnabas and Saul for the work to which I have called them.' Then, after fasting and praying, they laid their hands on them and sent them off." True worship inevitably issues in evangelism.

Similarly, that evangelism which does not lead to worship is an abortive activity. No longer may the phrase, "to snatch a brand from the burning," be regarded as a sufficient motive for evangelism. Parents who have a child and then abandon it may not be regarded as responsible, nor may that evangelism be considered Christian which concerns itself only to get "decisions for Christ" and is not troubled about what happens subsequently.

The goal of evangelism is not to make converts; it is to produce mature Christians. Jesus was precise in giving the Church her great commission. He sent the Church out, not to make converts, but to "make *disciples.*" The term "disciple" means "learner." Evangelism does not seek only to win men to Christ; it seeks to win them to Christ and the Church. Not to one or the other, but to both. Evangelists have often sought to make converts; ecclesiastics have often sought to make church members; neither is, in itself, enough.

Even as worship and evangelism are mutually indispensable, so there can be no separation of evangelism and Christian education. As was suggested earlier, many Christian educators tended in the past to regard nurture as a substitute for evangelism. Similarly many evangelists scorned the work of the Christian educator as lacking in definiteness. Again this compartmentalization of emphasis grows out of the failure to recognize the interrelatedness of Christian activity. Just as there can be no Christian evangelism unconcerned about nurture, so there can be no Christian education not evangelistically motivated. Commitment is both the goal and the point of departure in

Christian education. It is the goal when a child, having been instructed in the historic facts of the Christian faith, is brought to the point of decision and, with this background of information, is able to respond intelligently to God. Commitment is the point of departure in Christian education when an adult is won to the fellowship of the Church and is helped to develop his understanding of the Christian faith and the Christian life.

What is true of the relationship of evangelism to worship and Christian education is also true in such other concerns of the Church as stewardship, missions, and social action. Every area of activity in the Church must inform and be informed by evangelism or all will be crippled and incomplete.

IT IS not permitted for a minister to say "I am not an evangelist." . . . The minister is ordained for the purpose of bringing men and women to Christ; if he is not doing it, it is questionable whether he ought to be in the ministry at all. Equally, it is not open for a layman to say, "I cannot be an evangelist." If he is a Christian he must be a witness. If he is not willing to be a witness, it is time he gave up calling himself a Christian.

—STEPHEN NEILL

IV.
Toward a
Total Witness

FOR CENTURIES the principal responsibility for evangelism has been borne by the clergy. The laity were neither called to evangelistic activity nor believed it to be their responsibility. One of the most significant developments in the Church (possibly the single most important development in recent centuries) is the revival of lay activity and the growing recognition that the layman is called to a ministry no less important than that of the clergy. Elton Trueblood has said, "The Reformation opened up the Bible to the common man; a new Reformation will open up the ministry to the common man."

This increasing recognition of the importance of the layman has particular significance in relation to the Church's evangelistic task. It is a simple fact that if the clergy are to be the Church's only evangelists there is no possibility of an effective witness to the nation as a whole. It has been said that "If the world is to be won it will be won not by professionals, but by amateurs."

Even a cursory study of the Church and the world will reveal that a Church which delegates the burden of its evangelistic effort to the clergy is bound, by the very nature of things, to fail. There simply aren't enough pulpits or preachers. Even if the entire community were suddenly to decide to go to church (a highly unlikely occurrence) only a small proportion could get in. Inasmuch as this is not likely to happen, let us look at the situation in relation to the pastor. The fact is that the average pastor touches but a small segment of his community in a normal week's activity. On Sunday morning a captive audience of one hundred to two thousand people (almost all of whom are already related to the Church and predisposed to agree with whatever utterances he may make) sits before him. During the week he and the members of the teaching staff will address others, most of whom, again, are already at least nominally Christian. His work through the week is mostly related to the membership of the church. Therefore such contacts as he may be able to make through the services he renders and through normal social intercourse are relatively few and are usually anything but ideal evangelistic opportunities. It is a practical impossibility for the regular pastoral ministry to reach the great masses outside the Church who do not and are not likely to attend the regular preaching and teaching services.

Many labor under the illusion that the mass evangelist is the instrument for reaching the outsider. Unfortunately, the facts contradict. Surveys taken in Great Britain and in the United States reveal that more than 90 per cent of those present in the audiences of the foremost mass evangelists in the field today are or have been related to the Church. Not infrequently the figure runs as high as 94 to 96 per cent.

This fact is not to be construed as an argument against mass evangelism, for the Church itself must be evangelized. As has been said (perhaps unkindly), "The trouble with the Church is that half of her membership is unconverted and the other half is only half converted." The greatest benefit of mass evangelism has always been the change it effects in the lives of Christians. "Revival" means "a bringing back to life," and the mass evangelist renders his greatest service in reviving the lapsed and in bringing nominal Christians to some understanding of what is involved in Christian commitment. Unfortunately, most mass evangelists address 90 per cent of their remarks to 10 per cent of their congregations. If the mass evangelist speaks principally to the minority in his audience, most of the benefits of the mission will cease when he leaves; whereas if he seeks also to revive the Church, his departure will inaugurate increased activity as the Church begins to bear its witness through its revived membership.

It is clear that the Church's witness through its regular

activities and through special mass evangelism will, even if intensified, leave millions unreached. There is only one way the Church may reasonably hope to reach the outsider—through lay evangelism.

Significantly, this was one of the activities of the early Church and one of the reasons for its great penetration of Roman society. Lay evangelism had its origin when Jesus commissioned "the Seventy" and sent them out by twos. In a very real sense the Apostles were trained laymen who in turn won, trained, and sent out other laymen whose effective witness in the homes of others contributed much to the Church's phenomenal growth.

Subsequently, with the increasing distinction between the formal priesthood and the laity, the principal responsibility for the statement of the Christian message devolved upon the clergy. After the establishment of the Church in the fourth century, the "Christendom concept" destroyed much of the incentive for evangelism.

The Reformation restated the doctrine of the universal priesthood of believers but, while this effected a major difference in the relation of the laity to the sacraments and in other ways, it did not lead to any widespread ministry of evangelism by laymen. The Wesleyan revival developed many lay preachers and gave a sense of mission to the average Christian which had previously been absent. The "Great Awakening," the activity of such groups as the Quakers and the Salvation Army, and the emergence of revivalism in America called laymen in increasing numbers to bear witness to their faith. It has remained for our day, however, to impress upon the millions of men and women on the rolls of the churches that they too have been called to a ministry, different but no less important than that to which the clergy has been ordained.

There is an important distinction between the task of the clergy and the Church as a whole that is much misunderstood. In Ephesians 4 the Apostle Paul makes it clear that God gave the clergy for "the building up of the body of Christ." The first responsibility of the ordained minister is the care and nurture of his congregation. If this responsibility is adequately met, he and they together will evangelize the outsiders. The pastor is God's gift to the Church; the Church is God's gift to the world. The pastor's first responsibility is not to do evangelism but *to produce an evangelizing church.* The Church is the principal evangelizing agency.

This approach to the evangelistic task is not only New Testament in concept but feasible as to strategy. If the only evangelistic voice of a church is the pastor's, it is manifestly impossible to reach the community. But for every minister there are hundreds of members and, if even a small proportion of these are led into the bearing of their witness, a congregation will have not one voice but hundreds. Moreover, Church members are daily in contact with those outside who will not come within the door of a church. They rub elbows with the outsiders in business, in neighborhood activity, in labor unions, in places of recreation and in every area of concourse. Moreover, the layman's witness is frequently more effective than the clergyman's for it is unexpected; it being often held that "the minister is a paid salesman, the layman a satisfied customer."

Because the Church has failed to acquaint the laity with its ministry, two major misconceptions have arisen: first, the layman has felt that the witness of the Church is the responsibility of the clergy and, second, he has misunderstood his Christian vocation.

As a result of the first misconception, many a layman is resentful when it is broached that he bear his witness in an organized program of visitation evangelism. His frequent response is, "That's the minister's job. That's what we pay him for!" Erroneous as this may be, the clergy may not take umbrage, for the misconception grows out of the failure properly to instruct the layman in his responsibility as witness. "God was in Christ, reconciling the world to Himself . . . and hath given us the ministry of reconciliation." All are, in Paul's words, "ambassadors for Christ."

Bishop Stephen Neill of the Church of England has tersely stated the universality of the evangelistic calling:

It is not permitted for a minister to say, "I am not an evangelist." . . . The minister is ordained for the purpose of bringing men and women to Christ; if he is not doing it, it is questionable whether he ought to be in the ministry at all. Equally, it is not open for a layman to say, "I cannot be an evangelist." If he is a Christian he must be a witness. If he is not willing to be a witness, it is time he gave up calling himself a Christian.

The failure to acquaint the layman with his ministry has done him further disservice: it has deprived him of a sense of Christian vocation. The layman needs to understand that in the Protestant concept of work, you do *"whatsoever you do* to the glory of God." The layman's daily work (granted it is not reprehensible) is a vocation—a calling. The Kingdom and the world need Christian pastors, teachers, and evangelists, but they also need Christian doctors, lawyers, teachers, and others who regard their work as vocation and see it as an opportunity for ministry.

The double standard of commitment is a Roman Catholic concept and is contrary to the New Testament and the traditional Protestant view. Yet how many times are Christian young people called to "full-time Christian service"? The inference usually is that "full-time Christian service" applies, vocationally, to the ordained ministry or to service on the foreign field. In the Protestant concept, *all* Christians are called to an equal, total commitment that may express itself vocationally in many ways. Whatever your vocation may be, it is clear that you do *"whatsoever you do* to the glory of God."

The World Council of Churches, in the report of the Evangelism section at Evanston, stated:

The laity stands at the very outposts of the Kingdom of God. They are the missionaries of Christ in every secular sphere. Theirs is the task to carry the message of the Church into every area of life, to be informed and courageous witnesses to the will of our Lord in this world. To this end they will need training and guidance. Such training involves instruction in the content of the Christian faith and in the significance of that faith for obedience and witness in the different contexts of lay life. This kind of training will require the services both of ministers and of experienced laymen.

Having attempted to point out the importance of the layman as an evangelist, it is necessary to add a word of caution. The achievements of lay visitation have been so notable and so widely hailed that the Church is in danger of an uncritical adoption of the method. Beyond those stated above there are many obvious advantages to lay evangelism: it seems free of the excesses to which mass evangelism is subject, the costs of the program are negligible when compared to other special evangelistic efforts, the contribution made to the spiritual life of the participant is considerable, and it offers a means of reaching the person beyond the borders of the Church. However, those who enthusiastically recognize the potential in visitation evangelism must also face up to its possible misuse.

Oddly enough, the weaknesses of mass evangelism are the same weaknesses which appear in visitation evangelism. The mass evangelist was frequently criticized for presenting an inadequate, often fragmented gospel, for a preoccupation with numbers, for manipulating personality to achieve his own or ecclesiastical ends, and for failing properly to follow up the initial response. These are the identical errors to which visitation evangelism is subject.

The greatest weakness of lay-visitation evangelism lies in the inadequate training of the participants. Too frequently the visitors are sent out with little understanding of the task at hand and after but an hour or two of instruction. The instruction commonly is limited to a delineation of the method and to the inspiration of resolution in the timid. Suggestions are given as to how the common objections may be answered or circumvented. The remainder of the instruction period is usually spent in answering questions and relating instances in which reluctant laymen achieved remarkable results and came to consequent enthusiasm. Seldom is much instruction given about the nature of Christian commitment.

The very effectiveness of visitation evangelism is its greatest danger. And the method *is* effective; there are contemporary instances in which a single church added more than a thousand members in a single year through an intensive program of visitation. It is not difficult for the instructed layman to get signatures on Decision Cards. And there can be no doubt that many have been won to Christian experience through the method. However, despite the fact that the participants are specifically urged to seek commitments to Christ and not simply to proffer an invitation to the church, the average visitor is rather hazy on the distinction between Christian commitment and Church membership, and the urging has little practical effect. The natural tendency is to take the line of least resistance, and experience has shown that the vast majority of visitors make their invitation one to join the church and do not attempt the infinitely more difficult task of leading the person visited into a significant relationship with God.

While it is true that a man may bear effective witness to his faith with the first breath he draws after personally responding to God, it is also true that the earnest desire to become a fisherman for men does not, in itself, prepare the novice. Jesus spent weeks and months preparing his disciples before sending them out. The Church requires years of preparation before it ordains men to preach. Only an irresponsible church constantly organizes and sends out an untrained laity to do the work of evangelism. The goal of the Church is not success but usefulness. He does the Church no service who wins men and women to easy membership. One of the great weaknesses of the Church is its abundance of inactive members; the Church is not advantaged when it adds still more of them in a campaign principally concerned about numbers.

Visitation evangelism—as is true of every method of evangelism—is abortive unless it is followed with a long-term plan of nurture. The Church has always been careless in following up its evangelistic efforts. It is one thing to bring a babe to birth; it is an entirely different matter to raise a child to maturity. A concern which ends when the initial decision has been gained is no concern at all; it is the mere manipulation of personality to serve ecclesiastical ends and is, possibly, the greatest sin the Church can commit.

A woman in a Midwestern city was visited by a team of laymen who elicited from her the promise to be in church the following Sunday. She signed an application for membership under the impression she was agreeing to attend church. On Sunday she was startled to hear her name called out as one who was going to be received into the membership. Coming forward as requested, she stood with a group of others at the front of the church where she was asked to assent to a statement of faith. In company with the others she responded with a hesitant "yes," although the statement included assertions in which she did not concur, and was received into the membership of the church. Six months later, troubled by a feeling of guilt, she sought out another minister and confessed what she felt to be a sin in these words: "In the house of God, before the people of God, in response to questions asked by a man of God, I perjured myself . . . and thus became a member of the Christian Church."

It is impossible to overstress the importance of proper training for those who are to engage in visitation evangelism. The permanent effectiveness of the method depends upon the training of the layman, a thoughtful program of assimilation, and a conscientious follow-up. Anything short of this not only does a disservice to the Church and the world but will eventually produce the same reaction to irresponsibility that befell mass evangelism, losing it to the main stream of the Church for more than a generation. There is no finer or more legitimate expression of evangelism than lay visitation; it is personal, it is effective, and it is one of the areas in which the layman may express his ministry. However, it may also be used as the tool of the religious opportunist, and against this the Church must guard.

ALL BUSY ministers are faced with the temptation to plunder the predigested truths of dead sermon-makers, and there is the danger that the pressures of pastoral activity will so encompass some that, in seeking to fulfill their evangelistic obligations, they will take the line of least resistance and merely unearth the techniques and terminology of the past. It must be remembered, however, that it was precisely the techniques and the emphasis of the past that the Church rejected.

V.

From Such
Turn Away

IN A recent conference on evangelism a respected churchman made the comment, "We want evangelism back, but we want it full-orbed and Church-related." He was recognizing a fact (the current resurgence of evangelism) and voicing a fear: the fear that the Church may return to the kind of evangelism it repudiated a generation ago.

That there is a return to evangelism in the Church is evident. The expressions of this new-found concern are too numerous to list but include the establishment of a "Department of Evangelism" in every major denomination save one, the return of mass evangelism on a scale undreamed of, an increasing curricular emphasis on evangelism in the theological seminaries, a spate of books on the subject, a growing recognition of the place of educational evangelism in the church school, the deepening evangelistic thrust of University Christian Missions, the increasing use of the media of mass communication, and the venturing of the Church into unexplored areas of outreach.

The fear expressed in the churchman's comment grew out of misgivings as to some of the ways in which the current revival of interest in religion is being evidenced, and solicitude lest the resurgence take on the character of an "old-fashioned revival."

It is imperative that evangelism be restored to the heart of the Church, but the zeal which seeks to effect this end must be guarded lest it betray both evangelism and the Church. What is needed is not simply a return to evangelism, but a return to an adequate evangelism. It is well to clean house of the sterile intellectualism that in recent decades has been substituted for evangelistic passion, but it should be remembered that Jesus warned in vivid terms that the expulsion of an evil may lead to the intensification of evil to the point where "the last state . . . is worse than the first." The alternative to an evil may itself be evil (as witness the fact that the most vigorous voice raised against communism twenty years ago was Adolf Hitler's).

An adequate evangelism is impossible apart from an adequate theology. Many with great zeal for the practice of evangelism evidence impatience when it is proposed to study the evangelistic task. They tend to say, "let's quit talking about it and get on with it!" This impatience is understandable, for there are some who expend their total energy in discussion and never move to action. (Like the theological professor who was so busy proving the existence of God that he forgot to say his prayers). Nevertheless, any ultimately useful evangelism must be predicated upon comprehensive theological premises. This is not to suggest that the evangelist must have a doctorate in theology, but to assert that he must at least know what he is about and must be obedient to the biblical injunction to wed zeal to knowledge. As has been said:

> The last temptation is the great treason,
> To do the right thing for the wrong reason.

The danger, now that evangelism is fashionable again, is that the Church will repeat the errors of the past. One of the great benefits of the study of history is that in providing a record of mistakes in the past it enables us to avoid repeating them. It is frequently asserted that we need an "old-fashioned revival," by which assertion the speaker usually means a return to nineteenth-century revivalism. But this is precisely what we do *not* need.

There is always a group in the Church hankering for the "good old days" and for the "old-time religion." This nostalgia is symbolized in a chorus frequently sung in evangelistic meetings, "Give Me the Old-Time Religion," in which apostolic sanction is begged by asserting that

> It was good for Paul and Silas
> And it's good enough for me.

The difficulty here is that the "old-time religion" of their day was *not* good enough for Paul and Silas; indeed, these worthies turned away from it to commit themselves to the new and more comprehensive revelation of the nature and will of God in the person of Jesus Christ.

One would not make light of tradition, but the "old days" are not good simply because they are old. We do not need (as is often stated) "another Moody" or "another Finney"; what *is* needed is twentieth-century Christians with something of the same commitment and evangelistic passion of these men, but with the added insights that have accrued to our generation through the increased understanding of theology, psychology, sociology, and other fields of human knowledge. The gains effected through Biblical criticism, archaeological research, and a maturing theology must not be lost because someone raises the cry "We must have a revival!" It is not enough to love God with the "whole heart," the Church must love Him with the "whole mind" as well.

All busy ministers are faced with the temptation to plunder the predigested truths of dead sermon-makers, and there is the danger that the pressures of pastoral activity will so encompass some that, in seeking to fulfill their evangelistic obligations, they will take the line of least resistance and merely unearth the techniques and terminology of the past. It must be remembered, however, that it was precisely the techniques and the emphasis of the past that the Church rejected. An uncritical espousal of the old evangelism will do a great disservice to the Church and to the Christian cause. The old patterns may have a contribution to make, but they will not serve unless they have been brought under careful scrutiny and have had new meaning breathed into them.

What, precisely, were the mistakes of nineteenth-century evangelism which, for convenience, I shall refer to as "Fundamentalism"? The basic error is the denial of the intellect. Refusing to "love God with the whole mind," Fundamentalist theology suffers from arrested development. A faith that will not grow and expand tends to petrify.

The Fundamentalist erects a more or less arbitrary structure of theological thought and then superimposes it upon the facts. Each new fact is pressed into conformity with the preconceived pattern. As a consequence, with the passage of the years, the Fundamentalist becomes less and less given to self-criticism. A growing authoritarianism appears and manifests itself in an inquisitorial tendency, usurping the prerogatives of God and setting itself up as judge of the validity of the faith of others. Having fashioned his simple and static faith, the Fundamentalist now begins to see failure to conform to it as opposition to God.

Though apparently at the opposite pole from Romanism, Fundamentalism proceeds from similar judgments and falls into similar errors. Both see little likelihood of salvation apart from their fellowship. Papal infallibility finds its counterpart in a view of Biblical inspiration implicitly denying the real presence of the living God at the heart of the

Church and substituting, in Luther's words, a "paper Pope." The Fundamentalist, like the Romanist, tends to become the patron of Deity and presumes to state under what circumstances God is bound to act. He further seeks to do the impossible; to formulate perfectly a theology about God— a theological orthodoxy. Unfortunately, as George Buttrick has said, "the church that claims infallibility loses the privilege and catharsis of confessing its sins."

Fundamentalist evangelism not only oversimplifies the gospel, it oversimplifies the Divine-human relationship. The gospel is preached in terms of "a plan of salvation," each step of which may be ticked off and substantiated by proof texts. The world is divided into "the saved" and "the lost," the individual transferring from one group to the other upon "confessing his sins" and "accepting the Lord Jesus Christ as personal Savior." Salvation relates a man to God but not to the world; indeed, it very pointedly calls him out of the world.

The principal difficulty with this concept, apart from the fact that it is made up of Biblical half-truths, is that it fails to take into account the infinite differences in individuals and the infinite variety of ways in which God deals with men. With our limited understanding of God and His purposes, we dare not see life in terms of blacks and whites, nor may we divide the world simply into "the saved" and "the unsaved." Unless our view is entirely static, men and women simply will not fit into these categories. C. S. Lewis has written:

The world does not consist of 100 per cent Christians and 100 per cent non-Christians. There are people (a great many of them) who are slowly ceasing to be Christians, but who still call themselves by that name; some of them are clergymen. There are other people who are slowly becoming Christians, though they do not yet call themselves so. There are people who do not accept the full Christian doctrine about Christ, but who are so strongly attracted to him that they are his in a much deeper sense than they themselves yet understand.

Nineteenth-century evangelism falls into the further error of equating conformity with Christian experience. In consequence evangelistic preaching becomes principally a matter of techniques and terminology. The Fundamentalist confuses certain phrases and experiences with the gospel itself. A preacher is "sound" if he weaves into his discourse such phrases as "ye must be born again" and "accept the Lord Jesus Christ as your personal Savior," and makes reference to "the blood of Christ." If phrases like these are included in the sermon, the preacher is regarded as orthodox, even though he may not have preached the gospel at all. If he omits these phrases, he is categorized as a "modernist." Orthodox terminology and specific techniques in giving a gospel "invitation" become touchstones of orthodoxy. If they are present, the gospel has been preached; if they are absent, it has not.

It is interesting to note how unrelated this concept is to the evangelism of the New Testament. This static kind of orthodoxy was unknown to the early Christian preachers.

If the failure to use the terms and techniques listed above makes for what is loosely categorized as "modernism," then one must count Peter, Stephen, Paul, and others as "modernists." Nine "sermons" are reported, in more or less detail, in the Acts of the Apostles, some delivered to Jews, some to pagans, and some to the Christian community. Significantly, the phrases "born again" and "accept Christ as your personal Savior" are absent, nor is there any reference to "the blood of Christ." To be sure, the profound meaning of these phrases is conveyed. But the early preachers did not fall into the current error of elevating certain segments of the gospel and equating them with the gospel itself.

One might ask why, if the phrase "ye must be born again" is imperative to evangelistic preaching, did Jesus not use it again and again? Why did he not respond to the Rich Young Ruler's question, "What must I do to inherit eternal life?" by saying, "Ye must be born again"? Why did he not so answer the "lawyer" who put the same question? Why is there no mention of the phrase in the Sermon on the Mount, in his conversation with the Samaritan woman, or in his addresses to the crowds in Jerusalem? Why did Paul not speak it to Festus or to Agrippa or, at least, to the Greeks in Athens?

Beyond doubt these phrases have profound Christian significance, but only an impoverished and partial ministry would mistake the reiteration and embellishment of particular sayings for the preaching of the gospel. By all means let the Church call men to repentance that there may be born within them a new spiritual consciousness and a willingness to respond to God's will for themselves and the world, but let the Church eschew that casting of the unsearchable riches of grace into rigid little human molds.

Nineteenth-century evangelism further oversimplifies the challenge confronting the Church in the superstitious belief that religious revival will solve the great problems of the world. It naïvely presumes that the conflicts and hostilities between nations and men will automatically disappear if the men and women who make up these nations are converted to Christ. It envisions revival as capable of solving the differences between labor and management, between Negro and White, between Nationalism and Colonialism, between East and West. One of the prominent spokesmen for this approach to evangelism has said, "I believe with all my heart that if we would have a real revival, all the things which divide us would be worked out."

The error in this view is twofold: it forgets, first, that the great "revivals" of history did not resolve the problems of *their* time and, second, that Christian experience does not produce uniformity in outlook.

There can be no doubt that religious revival affects society in more than a narrowly religious way. A notable case in point is the Wesleyan revival which altered the moral climate of England and, through such individuals as Wilberforce, brought about many much-needed social reforms. It is, however, a kind of religious utopianism to hold that the conversion of great numbers of men and women will inevitably solve the problems dividing man from man and nation from nation. This is clearly evidenced in the divisions within the Church itself. Christians of equal piety often take radically different positions on specific issues. A man may be "converted" and a member of the Church and yet have areas of his life in which he is not converted. Christian experience does not produce perfect wisdom (or there would be no room for growth) and a man might be, for instance, a good Christian and a bad statesman. A man may be a Christian and yet have psychological maladjustments needing professional attention. Religious revival does not and will not automatically solve the problems which bedevil mankind, and it is vastly oversimplifying man's dilemma to hold that it will.

Nineteenth-century evangelism errs also in its apparent belief that the way to cure an ill is to denounce it. More will be said later as to the necessity for a positive proclamation of the gospel; suffice it to say here that the violent denunciation of specific sins is frequently dangerous. First, because it conveys the impression that Christianity is a negative faith principally concerned with the shedding of certain peripheral sins. Second, because it castigates the sin and the sinner without any recognition of the factors which have contributed to the problem. One may, for instance, hurl great thunderbolts at the drunkard with little recognition of some of the reasons why he drinks. An English laborer in a Manchester slum responded to an inquiry as to why he drank by saying, "I drink, your Reverence, because it's the quickest way out of Manchester."

Jung, the psychiatrist, has said, "Condemnation does not liberate, it oppresses." One wonders whether the fiery denunciations of some preaching and the constant emphasis on hell and judgment are not less the revelation of God than the revelation of unconscious resentments and hostilities, born of a deep sense of guilt, within the preacher.

A GREAT many methods (as diverse as the Religious Emphasis Week of the university campus and the pentecostalist "healing revival") are being used by the Church in its increasing emphasis on evangelism. Some are wholesome; some are fraught with peril. The encouraging feature is that individuals and denominations are casting about for new means by which the gospel may effectively be brought to the world.

VI.
Signs of
Resurgence

"EVANGELISM IS spoiled equally by attempts to change its message and reluctance to change its method." The store-front church which emblazons across its face, HERE WE PREACH FIRST-CENTURY CHRISTIAN-ITY, may believe it is being true to God; it is very probable that it is being untrue to its generation. Any significant return to evangelism must go beyond a mere parroting of the emphases of previous generations. In a lightning-footed century the Church must be abreast of its time even while it finds its resources in its historic faith. Effective evangelism proceeds from the understanding of two things: the gospel and the man to whom it is to be communicated.

It has been asserted earlier that there is currently a return to evangelism. While this is undoubtedly true, it must be understood that in a sense the Church has never ceased to be evangelistic. The Church is always within a generation of extinction. The Church militant would cease to be if its present members should die without winning others to follow in their train. It is obvious then that, if the Church is to perpetuate itself, it must be evangelistic. Evangelism is not an option; it is a condition of survival. The fact that the Church persists to this day is evidence that, across the centuries, it has been evangelistic. The question is not "Will the Church be evangelistic?" it always has been. The question is "What *kind* of evangelism will the Church do?"

Let us briefly survey some of the means by which the Church is at present seeking to express her evangelistic concern.

Official denominational concern may best be seen in the establishment of "Boards" or "Departments of Evangelism." As recently as 1940 only one major Protestant denomination had a full-time Secretary of Evangelism (The Presbyterian Church, U.S.A.); currently every major denomination save one (The Protestant Episcopal Church) has someone serving in this official capacity. Some denominational boards have large staffs and a sizable budget.

The activities of these boards are, by and large, almost identical. The programs developed by the various denominations are shared by correspondence and in a biannual meeting of the denominational Secretaries under the auspices of the Joint Department of Evangelism of the National

Council of Churches. Literature, program, and concepts are expounded, and the various leaders add to their own insights the experience and vision of their counterparts in other denominations. The result of this sharing is that the evangelistic programs of the various communions are essentially the same, varying only as they reflect particular doctrinal views.

The principal thrusts of the churches lie in visitation evangelism, pulpit evangelism, the care and assimilation of new members, and the deepening of the spiritual life of the Church. To the accomplishment of these ends an enormous literature has been developed, ranging in variety from motion pictures through filmstrips, books, turnover charts, pamphlets, leaflets and tracts.

The numerical gains directly traceable to the efforts of these denominational boards are often impressive. The enormous increase in membership of the Methodist Church, for instance, is, in a large part, due to the very intensive evangelistic thrust of that denomination in recent years. The membership index of the Presbyterian Church, U.S.A., registered an immediate upturn upon the initiation of what was termed the "New Life Movement" in that church. Other denominations have made comparable gains.

Certain denominations (e.g., some sections of the Lutheran Church), though unrelated officially to the National Council of Churches, have none the less borrowed much from the programs of the other communions. Southern Baptists, by and large, have relied upon pulpit evangelism, the annual "revival," and the more or less unorganized witness of laymen to accomplish their objectives.

The evidence leaves little doubt that in recent years the denominations have awakened to their evangelistic responsibility. There is increasing activity in the field and growing evidence that the challenge is being faced up to with vision and insight.

The present resurgence of evangelism is evident also in the theological seminaries. While there are notable exceptions, it may be said that the major theological seminaries have failed to provide adequate training in evangelism. Until recently many seminaries did not include the subject in their curricula. When courses were offered, they were often encompassed in a three- or four-hour elective. Only infrequently was evangelism a required subject for graduation. In the past decade this situation has been changing. Courses on evangelism are being added to the curriculum in many seminaries, and studies are being undertaken in an attempt to rethink the entire matter of the communication of the gospel to contemporary man.

The general failure of the seminaries to deal with the subject matter of evangelism has been a serious defect in the Church. The lack of comprehension of the evangelistic task and the ineptitude of many ministers in the practice of evangelism is directly traceable to a lack of instruction in seminary. One of the prerequisites to any significant revival in the Church is a revival of interest in the concept and practice of evangelism in the theological schools.

It must be stated here that some seminaries take the position that evangelism is implicit in every course offered, and that the absence of courses on the subject does not grow out of neglect so much as the conviction that evangelism is best served when it lies at the heart of every area of theological instruction.

In a sense this is profoundly true: evangelism *is* integral to every area of theological concern. For instance, church history encounters evangelistic practice in every era and can observe the benefits and the heresies arising from it from New Testament to modern times. Theology, concerned as it is with the nature of God and man and the relating of the one to the other, provides the ground from which evangelism proceeds. Preaching classes have as their primary aim the effective proclamation of the evangel to men. Christian education finds both its goal and its point of departure in commitment. The study of the denominations yields evidence of the enormous contribution evangelism has made to their emergence in history. New Testament studies reveal the central importance of the witness of the Church. In short, evangelism lies at the heart of all theological study.

It is not enough, however, to teach evangelism by indirection. This is clearly demonstrated in the general ineptitude of hundreds of seminary graduates in the matter of evangelistic preaching.

Serious study needs to be undertaken in many areas: the

place of evangelism in the Church, the nature of Christian commitment with particular reference to the varieties of Christian experience, New Testament expressions of evangelism and their relation to the contemporary task, the historical, sociological, and psychological factors bearing upon such significant events as the Wesleyan Revival, the "Great Awakening," the so-called "Welsh Revival," and others, the various causes underlying the response to Finney, Moody, Sunday, and, contemporaneously, Billy Graham, need to be brought under scrutiny. These and a host of related subjects require the attention of the acute, theologically grounded thinking possible only in the theological college. Only thus will the ministry of the future be equipped to witness with adequate intellectual comprehension and evangelical passion.

As a further result of the revival of interest in evangelism, University Christian Missions are being conducted in greater numbers and with a more immediate evangelistic emphasis. Something of the changed tenor of our time may be seen in the fact that university students, traditionally skeptical of and unresponsive to evangelism, are willing to give ear (if not necessarily to respond) to the Christian message. When the evangel is presented by a missioner equipped for this task, the response is often quite remarkable. Last year more than 350 missions were held in American universities and colleges. Many made a deep impress upon the student body and faculty.

A mission to university students calls for particular gifts in the missioner. In the academic situation, where the principal emphasis is on the cultivation of the mind, his message must be intellectually authentic and rationally acceptable. He must blend erudition and piety. No group in society is more sensitive to hypocrisy, cant, and pretense; nor is there any group so generously responsive to sincerity and to truth.

The gospel is to be addressed to the whole man (intellect, emotions, and will), but too frequently the appeal in university missions is directed almost entirely to the intellect. There is a great temptation in an academic situation to succumb to intellectual pride, to display one's erudition and to turn the Christian gospel into a Christian philosophy. There is, of course, a philosophical content to the Christian faith but, essentially, it is an evangel to be proclaimed, not an ethic to be defended. The preacher is not the formulator of a philosophy; he is the herald of an evangel. The missioner frequently forgets that his is a twofold task: he is both apologist and evangelist. He must not only make a response to the objections to Christian faith, but must seek to bring men's wills under the lordship of Christ. He must approach his task with an informed mind and eschew dogmatizing as he would the plague, but, ultimately, he must be prepared to preach the cross in the knowledge that it is "foolishness to the intellectual."

It is impossible accurately to reckon the value of a successful university mission. Graduates go from the universities to mold the character of the nation. Not only may converts be won to the Christian Church in a mission, but the shaky faith of confused Christians may be strengthened and given direction. The Church has regularly lost the allegiance of thousands of young people during their college years simply because they were not able to make the transition from a simple to a responsible faith. This ought not to be. Much is being done on campus by the various denominations to give counsel, instruction, and information to their own young people, but the impress of religious life on the average campus is not deep and needs a greater evangelistic thrust. The eventual ramifications of good campus evangelism are incalculable. The Christian Church should set up the necessary apparatus properly to employ such men as have the unique gifts needed for university missions.

The most frequently discussed aspect of the renewed interest in evangelism is the return of mass evangelism on a scale long believed impossible. Few thoughtful churchmen could have been convinced as recently as ten years ago that crowds of people numbering from five to one hundred thousand would gather night after night for evangelistic services not unlike those of Billy Sunday and Dwight L. Moody. In the years following Billy Sunday's heyday every article or book on evangelism read the obituary (sometimes rather gleefully) of mass evangelism. Mass evangelism, it seemed, was dead, and there was no power in earth or heaven which could resurrect it.

Indications are, however, that as with Mark Twain "the

reports were slightly exaggerated." In recent years evangelistic meetings have regularly outdrawn the largest sports events and political gatherings in North America and Europe. The fact is the more amazing when it is recognized that the largest crowds have gathered to hear a man who might accurately be described as standing in the tradition of Moody and Sunday; a man who denounces sin with great vehemence, preaches an imminent judgment and a literal Hell from an infallible Bible and concludes it by giving an altar call! It would seem fitting that the prognosticators in the religious field join the political pollsters and other prophets at a banquet of crow.

The return of the mass evangelist came as a surprise, for the past generation had been a barren one for him. Although a number of itinerant evangelists were active among some of the smaller denominations and with the nondenominational churches, few were known beyond their own immediate connection. "Gypsy" Smith continued his campaigns until his death at sea in 1949, but his was a declining ministry and was not attracting large numbers of people. The only other nationally known figure of the era was that extraordinarily complex woman, Aimee Semple MacPherson, who is anything but adequately described by the mere term "evangelist."

A new kind of mass evangelist, the so-called "radio-evangelist," emerged during these lean years. Dr. Walter E. Maier, a Lutheran of the Missouri Synod, spoke regularly over a network of radio stations reported to be the largest in the world at that time. Charles E. Fuller conducted "The Old-Fashioned Revival Hour," a weekly, nondenominational broadcast over a large network of stations. However, neither of these men conducted mass evangelism campaigns in the traditional manner and were given relatively little attention in the nation's press.

Dr. E. Stanley Jones was perhaps the best-known evangelist of the last generation. During his annual six months' absence from his missionary responsibility in India he conducted highly successful evangelistic missions in the United States and other Western nations. Dr. Jones does not, however, readily fit into the category of "mass evangelist." His interests have been many and varied. He is primarily a missionary and has labored at that task in India for years. As an author with a wide audience he has recently occupied himself in seeking what he terms "Federal Union" among the denominations.

A strong case could be made for the assertion that the greatest evangelist of the past generation was Harry Emerson Fosdick. Though doctrinally the antithesis of the mass evangelist, he spoke to great audiences in the Riverside Church and to millions on a nation-wide weekly radio broadcast. His more than two dozen books have reached into the lives of millions more. His influence, especially among university students and what someone has described as the "up and outs," has been enormous. There was an unmistakable evangelistic note at the heart of Fosdick's sermons and real evangelistic passion. It may be that, though anything but typical of his predecessors, he will be seen to have been the outstanding evangelist of his day.

The Reverend Canon Bryan Green, Rector of Birmingham, England, is the precursor of today's more traditional mass evangelists. Crowds ranging from two to twenty thousand people have nightly attended his meetings in the British Isles, Australia, Canada, and the United States. Green is not a full-time mass evangelist, spending the larger part of the year on his parish responsibilities and approximately three months annually conducting evangelistic missions under Anglican or Protestant Episcopal auspices. He first came to national attention in the United States as the result of a highly successful mission, in 1949, in the Cathedral of St. John the Divine in New York City. Attendances at a single service went beyond the ten thousand mark and he made a deep impression upon the Diocese and upon the city.

Canon Green is not the traditional mass evangelist; his theological approach, though conservative, is never obscurantist. He is strongly evangelical but, as might be expected, has a high doctrine of the Church. His preaching is positive, somewhat dogmatic, quite candid, and is delivered in a conversational tone. His sermons are studded with illustrations and frequently laced with humor. The invitation does not follow a set pattern and is not prolonged. Green and other members of the clergy do much personal counseling, which is followed up by the Diocese. An interesting and novel feature of Green's meetings is the "question period" during which the missioner answers written questions submitted by members of the congregation during the singing of hymns in the early part of the service.

Undoubtedly the best-known evangelist in the world today is Dr. William Franklin Graham, better known as Billy Graham. A Southern Baptist, Graham has drawn some of the largest crowds in religious history. He has equaled or topped Billy Sunday's attendances in every city where both have appeared and has spoken in person to as many as two hundred thousand in a single day.

By and large, Graham fits the pattern of the traditional mass evangelist. The themes of his sermons, the manner of their delivery, the theological concepts, and the invitation and afterservice techniques are similar to those employed by the best-known evangelists of previous generations. It is inevitable that Graham be compared to Dwight L. Moody and Billy Sunday. There are many similarities and many differences. His sermons are not so simple and direct as were Moody's, and he is given to more extravagant statement. On the other hand, he is not so flamboyantly dramatic as was Sunday.

Theologically, Graham is strongly conservative and a biblical literalist. There is, however, nothing of the intransigent about him. Beginning his ministry with nondenominational "Fundamentalists" he has moved constantly closer to the organized Church. Even those who disagree with his theology and his methods like him and admit to his sincerity. Graham has matured with his rise to eminence and has shed many of the eccentricities which, at first, militated against acceptance by many of the clergy. He no longer affects a flashy attire, no longer receives "love offerings," has diminished the dramatically emotional character of his invitations, and has ceased to make sensational eschatological predictions. Despite a torrent of publicity that has brought him to world-wide fame and made him the best-known Protestant minister in the world, Graham has maintained a remarkable humility.

Graham's sermons vary in length from forty minutes to an hour. The words "sin," "hell," "judgment," "repentance," "salvation," "born again," and "personal Savior" dominate. The most frequently used phrase is "The Bible says . . ." Graham has a deficient understanding of the nature of sin, a strong tendency to present conversion as a transaction, a tendency to ally God with America in a common opposition to Communism, and a rather naïve conviction that revival will resolve the world's great issues. On the whole, his message typifies the strongly conservative, evangelical Protestant view, and though the majority of the clergy in the major denominations would not entirely concur with Graham's theology or his methods, they are impressed with his earnestness and usually co-operate in his campaigns. Despite his enormous success, many churchmen have grave doubts about the ultimate value of his contribution.

One of the notable features of contemporary mass evangelism is the emergence of the "healing evangelist." In the past decade a number of men—most of them Pentecostalist

—have come to prominence through what are termed "healing revivals." The healing revival is similar in general approach to the tent meetings of former mass evangelists, but has unique features not previously seen in mass evangelism. The services are distinguished by what is called the "healing line." Converts with physical ailments, after rudimentary instruction, pass in a long line before the evangelist who questions them as to the nature and duration of their affliction, "lays hands" upon them, and prays for their healing.

The best known of the healing evangelists is an Oklahoman by the name of Oral Roberts. In his youth he was afflicted with stammering and claims to have been delivered from the affliction through "faith healing." (In simple reportorial accuracy it must be stated that he still occasionally lapses briefly into a stammer.) Following in the trail established by a number of healing evangelists, Roberts soon attracted large crowds and widespread attention. In a brief time he has created a large and complex organization to administer his many activities. He travels across the United States and Canada with a fleet of trailer trucks carrying an enormous tent and the furnishings necessary to seat approximately ten thousand people. In addition to his public meetings he has a weekly network radio program and produces a filmed version of his tent services which is shown on a large number of television stations. He publishes a magazine called *Healing Waters,* and is the author of a number of books. His week-night attendances rival Billy Graham's, and the scope of his work has made it a multimillion dollar enterprise.

There can be no doubt that the great crowds attending the various "healing revivals" are drawn by the healing aspect of the services. Most of the healing evangelists are inferior preachers and depend a great deal upon the highly-charged emotional atmosphere of the services. The excitement engendered when some of the afflicted appear to be healed is electric and sometimes leads to that kind of ecstatic shouting and gyration which characterized early American revivalism.

That so-called "healings" are effected in these meetings is beyond question. The question that needs to be asked is whether most of the cures have anything to do with what might strictly be termed Christian faith or whether they may not be more properly accounted for as release from afflictions which are psychosomatic and hysteric in nature.

Anyone who has observed the work of the healing evangelists is likely to be concerned about the amount of harm done by the total impact of a "healing revival." There are instances where crippled, paralyzed, and spastic children have had their braces removed or have discontinued muscular re-education and have, as a result, been permanently injured. Though the healing evangelist does not advocate it, many patients cease to use prescribed medicines in an attempt to "have faith" and subsequently worsen in their illnesses, sometimes to the point of fatality. There is the further problem of the disillusionment among those who have striven to "have faith" and have found their faith unrewarded. There is the hurt to the total Christian cause growing out of the primitive, anti-intellectualism typical of the healing revival, and there is the harm done by a casting of the major emphasis in preaching upon the physical to the detriment of the mind and the spirit.

That the Church has a concern in the matter of what might be described as "spiritual healing" is evident in the fact that many of the major Protestant denominations are engaged in study and experimentation in this area. The Church of England has ordained one of its number to practice a ministry of prayer for the sick. The Church of Scotland has (particularly in the Iona Community) been engaging in prayer for physical healing and has been doing research in the field. The Presbyterian Church in the U.S.A. has set up a General Assembly Commission to study the matter, as have a number of other communions. A spate of books on "spiritual healing" have recently appeared, with others in the offing.

Beyond those listed above, a great many other methods are being used by the Church in its increasing emphasis on evangelism. Some of them are wholesome and some are fraught with peril. It is impossible to treat them in detail here. Let it suffice to list some. The National Council of Churches is carrying on Preaching Missions to the men and women of the armed forces in the United States and abroad. Industrial Chaplaincies are increasing. Small Groups or

Cells are being formed in great numbers and are inviting into their midst many persons entirely unrelated to the Church. Television and radio are being imaginatively employed and increasingly directed at the non-Christian. Religious drama is being used both "legitimately" and in motion pictures to capture the interest of the unchurched. Religious literature has undergone a revolution and emerged in highly attractive and imaginative formats. Breakfasts for businessmen and noonday theater meetings are reaching many adults. Youth Caravans, "Jalopy Raids," and campus witnessing are touching large numbers on the high school level. The encouraging feature in the resurgence of interest in evangelism is that individuals and denominations are casting about for new means by which the gospel may effectively be brought to the world.

PASSION MUST return to the pulpit if the Church would hope to catch the attention of the world. In a world that dins the merits of a better soap or cigarette in a voice which might better have been reserved for the announcement of the annihilation of a quarter of the globe by atomic explosion, the merely logical, dry-as-dust statement of Christian truth will make no impact. If man's predicament is as urgent as the gospel indicates, no placid, perfectly contained rescue attempt will do. In a world enthralled by materialism it will take a struggle and a wrench to turn men toward God.

VII.

The Pulpit
Is the Key

AT THE center of Protestant strategy to win the world to Christian discipleship stands the pulpit. This has been so for centuries. Whether by direct statement or by reflection from the life of the laity, preaching is central to the witness of the Christian Church.

There are few opportunities for influence comparable to that afforded the minister who stands to address an audience —whether that audience be gathered before a pulpit, a lecturer's stand, or a television set. In these enviable circumstances he is entirely free to choose his subject and, by every means at his command, press his convictions upon his hearers. At least once every week, Protestant Christian spokesmen in the United States alone have an audience of more than twenty-five million people seated before them ready to give ear to whatever they may wish to say. No other cause has a comparable forum. (One wonders what the Communists, with their passions for indoctrination, might do with a similar opportunity!) Yet, that America is so often unchristian in her national life, and Christians are so untutored in their faith, would seem to argue that the opportunity is not being used to full advantage.

It is a fallacy to assert that people today are not interested in preaching. A good sermon, well delivered, still holds a fascination, even in our sensate age, jam-packed though it may be with television "spectaculars" and cinemascope movies. That millions can be interested in a religious address is attested to by the audiences which listen to the Roman Catholic Bishop, Fulton J. Sheen, in his weekly television show. Bishop Sheen insists, one must note, that his broadcast is not a "religious" program except in the sense that all of life is religious. (The distinction is a rather tenuous one, and the "talk," if that is what it must be called, sounds very much like a sermon. The point is that millions who would describe it as a sermon listen to it.) It is estimated that the Bishop regularly speaks to as many as sixteen million people —more than the entire Christian Church spoke to in the first three centuries.

As for face-to-face confrontation, mention has already been made of the great crowds that gather in outdoor stadia to listen to Evangelist Billy Graham. The significant thing is that they come to hear a sermon, frequently an hour in length and sometimes difficult to concentrate upon because of problems of acoustics and inclement weather.

The written "sermon" has also demonstrated its potential interest in the phenomenal response to the sermons of Peter Marshall and Norman Vincent Peale. Countless people have read the books by these men or read their contents in newspaper syndication and other reprints.

The particular emphases employed by the popular preachers noted above may be open to question, nevertheless, they demonstrate that sermons, as such, are not outmoded. The tragedy is that with such an instrument to hand the Church has often neglected it.

Preaching is not the mere statement of religious truth. Apart from the supernatural overtones, preaching is an art, and skill in preaching, like skill in any other art, is not easily acquired. One would not expect to become a competent pianist or vocalist or sculptor or writer without practice and discipline, yet many ministers expect proficiency in preaching to come without it. Good preaching takes time and effort. There are no short cuts.

Unfortunately, today's minister is so encompassed about by a multitude of responsibilities that he is unable to find enough time for proper pulpit preparation. The problem, however, is often of his own making. The common Protestant dependence upon a professional ministry and the consequent failure to harness the power of the laity means that the average minister is hard put to find even a minimum amount of time. The fact is that many clergymen doubt the layman's ability and will not train him or entrust him with specifically Christian responsibilities. Yet in truth, many tasks regularly assumed by the clergy could be better performed by laymen. The minister frequently argues that he does not have the time to train his laymen for Christian service, failing to realize that he does not have the time because he will not train the laity.

It is exceedingly difficult to preach effectively. The disciplines of reading, research, study, and preparation demanded of the skilled homiletician are rigorous, and when such a legitimate excuse as "Wist ye not that I must be about my Father's business" can be seized upon, there is a great temptation to neglect them. There are few ministers who could not (if it seemed sufficiently important to them) set aside and jealously guard specific periods in the week to be used for preparation for preaching. The remonstrance, "I can't afford to give it the time," might be answered, "Can you afford *not* to?"

The man who insists upon his right to preach, but who will not bring to the task a prepared mind and relatively finished skills, fails the cause he espouses. He need not be expert in every field, but he must be willing to spend the time and energy to keep abreast of and work out a synthesis of modern knowledge sufficient to prevent himself from appearing ridiculous in intelligent company. It is true that unlettered men have occasionally caught the ear of the nation and made a profound contribution to the Christian cause, but such cases are the exception. Such men have usually been debarred from formal training by circumstances rather than choice, have given themselves diligently to self-culture, and have possessed the only substitute for the discipline of preparation—prodigious natural ability. This generation is not long going to take heed of the slovenly thinker. As Bishop Oxnam has said, "Our generation will not be led spiritually by men it cannot respect intellectually."

But effective pulpit evangelism will take more than an informed mind; it will take passion. There is too little passion in the contemporary pulpit. In place of passion we have substituted dignity, which is not quite the same thing. An anonymous reporter, having attended divine worship in a great American church, wrote the following report:

One felt as if the preacher had gathered a little loose talk around a subject which itself had no greatness in it. He spoke faultlessly, harmlessly, aimlessly. All that he said might be so, but it did not grip or fasten the attention, made no form of spiritual appeal, awoke no deep or answering emotion, and left the hearers as untouched as it found them.

One need not endorse that frantic, perspiring fulmination born of the assumption that what it lacks in lightning it can make up for in thunder, in order to deplore that casual kind of preaching which speaks of God and eternity with the same dispassionate voice one might use to dictate a laundry list. If there is any temptation to which enlightened preaching seems subject, it is the tendency to be casual; to preach with a here-is-the-truth, take-it-or-leave-it attitude.

Dispassionate preaching is sometimes a matter of temperament and training. More often it is born of a lack of a sense of urgency concerning the gospel. The informed preacher does not see life in easy categories. He is aware of the complexity of the problems to which men are subject and cannot brush aside with pat little panaceas the difficulties raised by the real confrontation of life. He would provide answers, but he fears charlatanism. He finds that the more thoughtfully he looks at life the more his integrity drives him to a reverent agnosticism about many things. His basic convictions may remain unshaken, but they are constantly under review and sometimes have to be reformulated. He is caught in the dilemma that bedevils the intelligent man: a reluctance to be dogmatic. As a consequence he sometimes loses the sense of urgency from his preaching—the sense of "Right here! Right now!"

Nevertheless, passion must return to the pulpit if the Church would hope to catch the attention of the world. In a world that dins the merits of a better soap or cigarette in a voice which might better have been reserved for the announcement of the annihilation of a quarter of the globe by atomic explosion, the merely logical, dry-as-dust statement of Christian truth will make no impact. If man's predicament is as urgent as the gospel indicates, no placid, perfectly contained rescue attempt will do. In a world enthralled by materialism it will take a struggle and a wrench to turn men toward God.

This is not a plea for that cheap burlesquing of legitimate

passion so often a part of evangelistic preaching. There is a sense in which it may be said of these that "their zeal hath consumed them." Their very vehemence forces them to maintain inertia by an ever-increasing sensationalism. The Japanese have a proverb which describes the dilemma: "He who rides the tiger dare not dismount." There is, however, a normal passion born of the Christian imperative which catches the preacher up and carries him beyond the mere presentation of religious discourses. We sometimes wonder why our people are not moved; may it not be because *we* are ourselves unmoved?

The cardinal sin of preaching is dullness. Dullness in the preacher is a greater sin than unspirituality, bad exegesis, or shoddy homiletics, for the preacher's first responsibility is to get the attention of his audience. It makes little difference whether he is a saint, a biblical scholar, and a skillful exegete if he does not have the attention of his audience.

It seems incredible that one of the commonest criticisms of the Church is that its preaching is often boring and dull. That the gospel should bore anyone is astonishing. It speaks to all of the problems and facts of life and offers as its answer the most vital and revolutionary Person the world has ever seen. It is a sin against all that is holy to transform the dynamic stuff with which the Christian preacher deals into the pallid, innocuous moralism so often passed out from the pulpit in the name of the Christian gospel. It is no easy thing to make the gospel dull, and it is a tribute to our ability that we can do it. Assuredly we could not, were we not able to borrow from a long tradition of dullness.

Unhappily, the Church has often managed to convey the impression to many beyond her membership that, while religion is important, it is tedious. Somehow, in our reflection of him, Jesus has emerged as a gentle, unreal, hopelessly impractical idealist, utterly unlike the dynamic and revolutionary figure he was. The Christian life has frequently been presented as a series of negative and debilitating prohibitions that one is to countersign. That the gospel should bore anyone is incredible. Dorothy Sayers has said, "The Christian faith is the most exciting drama that has ever staggered the imagination of man. We may call it revelation or we may call it rubbish; but if we call it dull, then words have no meaning at all."

Dullness in preaching and the consequent failure to reach our generation stems from numerous causes. Many a young minister emerges from the theological seminary full of promise only to succumb to the subtle temptation to intellectual pride. Unless one guards against it, the pulpit can become a platform for the parading of one's intellectual finery. Many a gifted young evangelist has lost his drive through a fear of being identified with the naïve and over-zealous group commonly referred to as "evangelistic." Many a sermon comes to be prepared with more concern for the impression it will create than the response it will win. Every pastor is subject to the temptation to fashion his sermon in such a way as to impress a particular group in his congrega-

tion (a university professor, an English teacher, a newspaper editor, a wealthy and influential businessman) for
whose views the minister has respect and whose approval he
desires.

The desire for intellectual respectability is a snare. It can
drive a wedge between a pastor and a great segment of his
congregation. It can kill the evangelistic passion. Some sermons are so filled with learned quotes and literary allusions
that they are actually not sermons but essays. A sermon must
never merely be literature; it is, primarily, communication.
A sermon may fascinate, inform, and inspire, but if it fails
to communicate divine truth it has failed. In Phillips
Brooks' famous definition, "Preaching is truth through personality," and, any embellishment which hinders the communication of that truth is out of place. There is no excuse
for slovenly homiletics or indifferent preparation, but if the
literary flavor of a sermon interferes with the lucid statement of Christian truth it is extraneous. It may be good
writing, but it is bad preaching.

Another reason why the Church has not reached this
generation with the preaching of the evangel is the failure
to formulate and state the gospel in understandable terms.
There is a sense in which every generation must rediscover
the entire gospel. The Christian heritage is matchless, but
only those truths are truly ours that have been validated in
our own experience. We are to "put on the whole armor of
God," but we must also "prove" that armor; Saul's armor
would not serve David in his task nor will yesterday's

theology and yesterday's insights automatically serve us in ours.

Much preaching slavishly follows traditional patterns. There is an enormous amount of good preaching in the contemporary pulpit, but also a staggering amount that is uninspired and just plain dull. Our tendency is to echo the terms we have inherited, but words, like faces and figures, have a way of changing with the passage of the years. It is so easy to run through the clichés (of which the Church has an abundance) without ever taking the trouble to think them through. Said Emerson, "We are students of words; we are shut up in schools and colleges and recitation rooms for ten or fifteen years and come out at last with a bag of wind, a memory of words—and do not know a thing."

How frequently the preacher uses archaic words and an outmoded terminology. The language may be pregnant with meaning to the preacher, but have little significance to the listener. It is an unwarranted assumption that the average churchgoer understands the fundamental concepts underlying the Christian gospel. The degree of ignorance concerning the fundamentals of the Christian faith is far greater than commonly supposed. It is a wise premise never to overestimate the religious literacy of an audience nor to underestimate its willingness to respond.

The need to state the gospel in terms meaningful to this generation is even more evident when one notes that 40 per cent of the total population of the United States has no church relationship of any kind. Many of them are, in

Elton Trueblood's phrase, part of a "cut-flower civilization" with some immediate connection to a generation familiar with Christian ideas. It may be presumed that, even if their views are hazy, they have had at least a secondhand contact with the Church. But what of the generation coming into being? More than seventeen million children in the United States are receiving no formal religious education. To presume that when they come to years they will find the utterances of the Church significant is to indulge in the most irresponsible kind of wishful thinking.

One is not arguing, of course, for a blithe casting away of all that is unintelligible to the non-Christian and for a descent into jargon. If a generation can learn the complicated terminology of psychoanalysis and weave such terms as "repression," "guilt complex," "id," and "schizophrenia" into its daily conversation, it can surely be expected to accommodate itself to the well-worn coin of theological and biblical terminology. What is being argued is that the Christian must face the realities of our culture and, without abandoning the traditional language of the Church, strive in every possible way to make it significant to the non-Christian.

That there are dangers at the point of seeking to "speak to the man in the street on his own level" is evident. It can easily lead to unbecoming excess. One shudders at the recollection of hearing the thrice-holy God addressed as though He were "one of the boys" with Whom the preacher was on terms of buddy-buddy intimacy. To make the gospel lucid it is not necessary to employ slang or slovenly English. The goal is not accommodation to the linguistic practice of a generation but statement in terms that have meaning to the hearer. Communication is a tricky thing at best, as any minister knows by the unrelated comments about sermons made at the door after a service. To convey the gospel with power and insight to the average man in the pew is an infinitely difficult thing to do and even more difficult when we address the non-Christian. Every minister needs occasionally to be reminded that "shooting over the head of the audience is not a demonstration that you have superior ammunition, but rather that you have poor aim."

The reason much preaching is unintelligible and soporific is that its meaning is not clear in the preacher's mind. Much that passes for "deep" preaching ("It was a marvelous sermon, although I must say I didn't understand it. He certainly is deep!") is actually the result of fuzzy thinking. Has preaching ever been so profound as in the Sermon on the Mount? The wisest cannot plumb its depths, and yet a child can grasp its meaning. Press the fervent pulpit orator as to exactly what he means by some of his reiterated assertions, and he will often be hard-put to explain his meaning. Let a man ask himself what, *precisely,* he means when he speaks of "the will of God," or "the inspiration of the Scriptures," or "salvation from sin," or "the atonement." One recognizes, of course, that here we are face to face with the "mysterium tremendum" and can never fully grasp the meaning of these truths, but it would seem that the Christian minister is bound at least to try to think through the central assertions of his faith to the limits of his finitude. How many times we beg the legitimate questions with the pious suggestion that the questioner "accept it by faith." Formal theological training is not enough. A Christian minister must have more than what someone has termed a "gossip theology"—little snippets and patches of the thinking of other men ("Barth says this" and "Niebuhr says this") picked up by reading. Second-hand convictions are juiceless things.

Another reason for the failure to reach this generation with the preaching of the evangel is the failure to understand our generation. The implications of the incarnation in the life of the minister need to be more fully understood. Some have little sense of identification with great segments of society and consequently little understanding of them.

It has been said that "the Church is like the world and yet out of touch with the world." It is a fact that there *are* clergymen who are out of touch with their generation. Some evangelicals, because of the fear of defilement by what they rather ambiguously refer to as "the world," grow progressively more isolated from their contemporaries. A kind of ministerial "professionalism" causes others to assume a self-conscious religiosity that puts all with whom they come in contact ill at ease. Some ministers affect a sort of "preciousness" that is repugnant to non-Christians. It was said of one minister, "He's a good brother . . . but he's also a good sister."

But there is an opposite pole: the minister who is too *like* his generation. He may be the "hail fellow, well met," the jovial, back-slapping "man among men" who seems always to be under a compulsion to prove that for all the fact that he is a minister he is a real man, or he may be the literate, "easy mixer" who has substituted culture for the evangel. Thomas Merton relates, in *The Seven Storey Mountain,* how, as a jaded young student, in an agony of spiritual confusion and hungering for a crumb of Christian certitude, he used to attend a Protestant church in New York City:

The minister of the church was very friendly and used to get into conversations about intellectual matters and modern literature, even men like D. H. Lawrence with whom he was thoroughly familiar. It seemed he counted very much on that sort of thing—considered it an essential part of his ministry. That was precisely one of the things that made the experience of going to his church such a sterile one for me. It was modern literature and politics that he talked about; not religion and God. You felt that the man did not know his vocation, did not know what he was supposed to be.

It must be remembered that Merton has a bias, but it must nevertheless be admitted that his picture is not an entirely inaccurate portrayal of some clergymen. There are some who are long on matters "spiritual" and short on any real understanding of their fellows; there are others who are so like their fellows that they cannot lead them beyond friendship.

The Christian answer to the gap between the Church and the world is the incarnation. The Christian evangelist must proceed from his relationship to God to identify himself with the non-Christian whom he seeks to win. There can be no simulating of rapport. He must have a genuine compassion, a compassion kept from being "sickled o'er" with condescension by the constant memory of "the pit from which he is digged." There is too great a distance from the pulpit to the public square and from the pew to the market place. Jesus was deity incarnate and yet fittingly described as "a friend of sinners." The clergy follows in his train.

The effective evangelistic preacher must be the student of the drives and hopes and fears of his generation. In this "the children of this world are wiser than the children of light." For purely commercial reasons, manufacturers and publishers pay large sums for surveys purporting to reveal the likes and dislikes of the nation. If a new product is to be marketed or a new package given to an old product, segments of the nation are sampled for their opinions, psychologists test the reactions of particular groups, and every possible means to discover the attitudes of the public is employed. The desires of the consumer are brought under careful scrutiny and then catered to in order to merchandise the product.

One would not suggest that the Church ever pander to the desires of men, but surely the "children of light" must seek to be as wise in their understanding of the drives and hopes and fears that motivate people. One wonders if a minister would not be well advised to listen to some "soap opera" and a few hours of rock 'n' roll; to read some of the inanities that pass for literature—not in search of material for a moment's satire with which to enliven a point in next Sunday's sermon, but as an open-minded student seeking to understand what human hungers and drives are finding some kind of fulfillment in such things. It is easy to condemn the eccentricities in a generation's taste; it is often difficult to recognize such things as some of the timeless urges within the spirit of man masquerading in modern forms. Such things must be understood if we would bring the gospel to bear upon this generation with insight and pertinency.

All of the foregoing would seem to suggest that it is imperative for Protestants to recognize and take advantage of the enormous potential in preaching. The preacher who speaks to this generation need never fear that he has nothing relevant to say or that there is no hunger to hear him. In all the long and turbulent history of the world the gospel has never been more pertinent than it is today. In a world where everything is relative many are listening for a voice to cry, "Thus saith the Lord God." It must be a voice that is authoritative without being dogmatic, a voice that is positive but not pontifical, a voice that is uncompromising but charitable. The preacher must inform even as he must inspire. His preaching must be biblical and historical, speaking the ancient wisdom of the Church, but it must also be relevant and practical. His sermons must be interesting, but never a mere collection of quotes and quips and epigrams that sound as if they were written with Bartlett's *Quotations* open at one elbow and *The Reader's Digest* at the other. It will be great preaching; not simply because it is profound in content and persuasive in delivery, but because it communicates the eternal Word of God to the heart of contemporary man with illumination and with power. The pulpit lies at the heart of Protestant strategy to win the world to God. Jesus said, "Go ye into all the world and preach. . . ."

BECAUSE MANY have not understood Christ's deity, or have been afraid of it (or have doubted it), they have tended to fall into the preaching of mere ethical homilies rather than the Christian gospel. They argue long and earnestly for Christian principles and fail to realize that there are no Christian principles worth getting excited about apart from Christ. The principles so frequently exalted have little meaning in themselves; what validates them is the authority of Christ. And he has no particular authority, if he is not, as he claimed to be, deity.

VIII.
Direction
for Tomorrow

TOMORROW'S EVANGELISM must be closely related
to the Church. Much of the evangelism of the past (especially mass evangelism) has been deficient at this point.
"There has been too great a gap between the tent and the
temple." The goal of evangelism is to win men to Christ
and the Church; not to one or the other, but to both. As
George Sweazey has put it, "The sawdust trail that does not
lead to a communion table is a blind-alley."

It is impossible to overemphasize the importance of the
Church in evangelism. The Church is not only the fellow-
ship of the redeemed, it is the redeeming fellowship. The
Church is at one and the same time the saved and the saving
society. The society into which the convert is won is the
Church.

The Church lies central to the evangelistic task. God in His providence has purposed to reveal Himself in history and to preserve the record of that revelation through the Church. The Church is to be the mirror of the love of God and the extension of the incarnation. The successful accomplishment of the Church's task is essential to the well-being of the world, for the Church is the single greatest influence for good. The Church informs government, the home, education, commerce and every other area of life. When the Church speaks with uncertainty or fails to be a redemptive force at the heart of a society there is an inevitable moral decline. The most important thing that happens in any community any week in the year is the gathering together on any Sunday morning of those who believe in God to worship Him.

Unfortunately, many evangelicals have had almost no doctrine of the Church. A great number have, in fact, occupied themselves with a constant sniping at the Church. Some have made their criticism the very ground of their existence. Asserting the utter and hopeless apostasy of the Church, they have withdrawn to independency. Most of the modern revivalists and the vast majority of the thousands of "tabernacles" that have sprung up across the country are unrelated to and often hostile to the organized Church. They are "one man shows"—the evangelist owning to no church allegiance and submitting to no discipline. This must be extraordinarily confusing to the non-Christian who expects Christianity to have some connection to the Church, however distant.

It is to be doubted that the independent has thought through the inferences of his self-imposed isolation. Arguing the necessity for isolation on the ground of the maintenance of true Christianity, the independent is, himself, the denial of his reason for being. The very reason he gives for independency (loyalty to Christ) is destroyed when he becomes independent, for independency is inevitably the expression of pride. The independent says by his action, "I alone am right. I alone, in all the world, have the truth and am obedient to it. Every Christian communion is wrong, and I cannot be associated with any of them. I cannot 'fellowship' with Presbyterians or Methodists or Episcopalians or any other group for they all are wrong. 'God, I thank thee that I am not as other men are!' "

Much of the opposition among evangelists to the organized Church grows out of a failure to understand the Church's essential nature. The critic of the Church who separates himself from it because of its imperfections is simply ignorant of what the Church is. The Church is a society of sinners, the only organization in the world where one of the conditions of membership is that you must admit you are imperfect. There is no room in the Church for the man who feels he is perfect. The Church welcomes only sinners. The Church is made up of men and women who recognize their imperfections and, having come to trust their lives to God through Jesus Christ, join hands with others like themselves, the better to worship and witness. The Church "in time" is imperfect; how could it be otherwise when it is made up of men and women? Independency is a betrayal of Christ, however good the stated intention, for if the message the independent preaches is the gospel of Christ despite the evangelist's imperfections, the Church is the body of Christ despite her sins.

The independent evangelical usually proceeds from a number of illusions. The early Church is romanticized and seen as a vital and deeply dedicated group, while the contemporary Church is hopelessly apostate. This common view is, however, contrary to the facts. When allowance is made for the differences in time and circumstance, the contemporary Church is not at all unlike the early Church.

Take, for instance, Jesus' little band of twelve. Were they, as a group, exemplary in a manner that sets them apart from today's Church? Hardly. Their "treasurer" was such a scoundrel that he betrayed his leader for a price and then in a fit of remorse committed suicide. (What a lurid scandal it would be and what headlines it would produce if the treasurer of Old First Church in Anytown, U.S.A., should betray his pastor for a bribe and subsequently leap from the top story of the Citizen's National Bank!) The second-in-command of that little church of twelve turned craven in a crisis and repudiated his Friend and Mentor with blasphemy. All of the little group elbowed and jostled each other at their last meal together, wrangling over prestige, and later, under fire, they "all forsook him and fled." A pretty sorry record!

—but who would not wish to have belonged to that heroic little band?

Or take as a further example, the early Church. Was it perfect? Well, two of its members were Ananias and Sapphira. Moreover, it had factional trouble: "there arose a murmuring of the Grecians against the Hebrews" concerning the disposition of food in its early communal system. It had a serious difference of opinion in the "Board of Foreign Missions" concerning the personnel of the second missionary team and "the contention was so strong among them that Paul and Barnabas departed asunder one from the other." There was a clash between the two leaders of this pristine Church that ended when Paul "withstood him [Peter] to his face." If any believe the early churches to have been pure and faultless congregations, each working with singleness of purpose to achieve the common goal, let him read the letters written to these churches and note the delineation of the sins being committed by the members— many of them sins a contemporary congregation would not countenance for a moment.

But weighing the relative merits of the early and contemporary Church would be a pointless task. What is more relevant is that the easy critic of the contemporary Church does not realize (or does not *want* to realize) that the Church has never been, at any point in history, much different than it is today. There have *always* been the dedicated and the indifferent, the humble and the proud, the zealous and the apathetic.

The Church needs critics; but they must be critics who love the Church. Dissent within the Church is not disloyalty. Judgment must begin at the house of the Lord. It is easy to snipe at the Church; its faults are many and need correction, but they will never be corrected by that constant, carping disparagement that does not hope to effect improvement but has simply grown professionally censorious. The sins of the Church may be corrected by those who love it enough to cry against its failures from within, having a stake in its welfare, while pointing to a better way.

It may further be said that without the Church we would not know of Christ; there is scant record of him in profane history. Our information about the historic Christ, his life and his teaching, comes from the Bible and the Bible comes to us through the Church. To believe that a man can come to Christian faith or preach or build a Christian congregation apart from the Church is to betray a woeful ignorance of the facts of history. God has seen fit to perpetuate the revelation of Himself and His will through the Church, unworthy as it is, and whether we like it or not we cannot escape it.

Tomorrow's evangelism must present a total gospel. One of the problems in evangelism is the achievement of balance. The evangelical who would properly serve his cause and the people to whom he ministers must sound every note in the scale of Christian values. This is seldom done. Some preach a strongly individualistic gospel with little reference to corporate sins and involvements. Some have a broad social compassion but evince little interest in personal religion.

One of the commonest failings in evangelistic preaching is the preaching of a predominantly negative gospel. It is particularly true when the preacher is addressing himself to non-Christians. Too often evangelistic preaching is distinguished by its thumping of the "thou shalt nots." Christian living is portrayed as inhibited, negative, restricting, and dull. One is a Christian because one has acquiesced to certain propositions about God and has left off doing certain reprehensible things. George MacLeod puts it this way:

The man of humor thinks if he becomes a Christian he will have to cultivate solemnity. The man of ambition that he will have to forget his dreams. Many a man of business thinks that he will have to resign his occupation and buy a tambourine. Many a youth thinks of Christianity as a long list of negatives to be countersigned and gloomily lived by.

In reaction to this negative aberration of the Christian gospel, many young people cry, "Become a Christian? I should say not! I will not live my life shackled and inhibited by a thousand ancient restraints!"

This negative presentation rises out of a faulty understanding of the nature of the gospel. Much modern evangelism proceeds on the assumption that "repentance and the remission of sins" is the burden of the gospel, which it is not. This was the message of John the Baptist and, although encompassed within the New Testament message, it is not the gospel. The mere announcement of forgiveness on the ground of repentance is negative. It has to do with the past and not the future. It frees a man from the guilt incurred by past misdeeds, but gives no assurance that he will not fall into the identical snare from which he is now released.

The Christian gospel goes beyond the announcement of forgiveness on the ground of repentance; it proclaims also that God will go with the individual into the future and will grant him the enablement to yield obedience. It not only calls *from* a way of life but *to* "abundant life." The note of repentance must never be lost from evangelistic preaching, for it is the ground of entrance into the life with God, but if it becomes the principal emphasis and Christianity is portrayed as a paring off of particular wrongs, then the "good news" becomes "bad news" and Christianity a denial of life.

Predominantly negative preaching arises not only from a faulty understanding of the nature of the gospel but from a misunderstanding of the nature of sin. Sin is seen, almost entirely, to consist in the performance of reprehensible acts. It is seldom seen as a failure to be—a "coming short" of the will of God.

Most evangelistic preaching speaks much of "sins" and seldom of "sin"—that fundamental self-sufficiency of which the acts are but a manifestation. There is much railing against drunkenness, sexual immorality, blasphemy, lying, smoking, card playing, and "the unpardonable sin" (which, by some kind of exegetical legerdemain, became refusing the evangelist's invitation on the closing night of the campaign). There is seldom any mention of corporate sins or any awareness of the individual's involvement in the great social ills of our time. Consequently, the converts tend to be converted only in certain areas of their lives and frequently accept the *status quo* on such matters as racial discrimination, economic injustice, slum housing, and commercial exploitation.

There are great dangers in a negative presentation of the gospel (as will be pointed out in the section on "Preaching for a Verdict"). It need only be stated here that any adequate New Testament evangelism must go beyond a predominantly negative emphasis.

A balanced, New Testament evangelism must go beyond a purely individualistic emphasis. It is not enough to seek to save a man's soul; men are not disembodied spirits and are not converted in a vacuum. The convert needs to understand that the Christian life consists not only in loving God with all of one's heart but also one's neighbor as oneself. Most evangelistic preaching (and, indeed, most evangelism) is deficient at this point. Often evangelism begins and ends with the "decision for Christ." Unless it begins there, it has not begun; but if it ends there, it has not properly begun. Too often the call to commitment is an appeal to escape the judgment of God and prepare for the world to come. The Christian life and its relationship to the world in which it must be lived is neglected. It is tragic if a man dies without Christ; it is doubly so if he *lives* without Him.

This great concern for conversion with little concern for sanctification emerges from that false dichotomy which has bedeviled the Church and militated against its usefulness: the concept that man is body and soul and that the Church is interested only in his soul. Not only is this a fundamental misreading of the New Testament, but it leads to a so-called "spiritual" preaching—an other-worldly "pie in the sky" attitude that has caused multitudes to look elsewhere than to the Church for the amelioration of injustice and inequity. The Church is obligated to the whole of man and not just the soul of man.

Have evangelicals really begun to relate their theology of the Incarnation to the work of evangelism? We remember Calvary, but do we remember Bethlehem? At Bethlehem "Jesus was made man" that he might identify himself with man and, by entering into man's life, redeem it. We are shocked that Deity is made to be born in a stable, and sense in the story that Jesus, by being born in these ugly and impoverished surroundings, is challenging the rightness of *any* child's being born into blighted surroundings.

The religions of the world in every age have said that God was to be found by turning away from the affairs of the world; Jesus came to declare God's presence in a carpenter shop, in the market place, and in the common meal. Surely this is the essence of the "inasmuch" story. Jesus taught that if men would serve him, they may do it by serving the unfortunate of earth. According to Jesus, he looks out of the eyes of the poor, the sick, the unhoused, the hungry. If we would visit him, we must visit the needy, the criminal, the dispossessed. "Inasmuch as you have done it unto one of them," he said, "you have done it unto me."

The Church is not other-worldly; it is interested in creating a better world *here*. It is not enough to "save souls" or convert people unless that conversion implies the conversion also of conditions that war on human well-being. It is true that good conditions are not the guarantee of good men, but it is also true that bad conditions breed bad men. Any Christian who has had to deal with children raised in slum conditions (where they have known nothing but ugliness and filth from the day of their birth) knows how sometimes their environment has so twisted and warped them that it is almost impossible to effect a response. So to speak, one puts a "hook" into the child in order to draw him gently toward God, but there is no moral fiber and the hook comes on through as though through jelly. Ralph McGill has pictured a teenage delinquent standing in court before a judge with the youngster giving new meaning to Luther's words as he says, "Here I stand. I can do no other."

The Church cannot hope to fulfill its evangelistic task around the world unless it demonstrates its concern about the conditions that warp and destroy human personality. Many of the gains of communism have come, not so much out of their achievements as from our failures. Communism prospers less by its theories than by capitalizing upon indignation. Dr. Charles Malik of Lebanon said at Evanston:

The great stirrings (in Asia and Africa) for social justice, for the elimination of discrimination and misery, for the liberation of the eternally depressed and dispossessed, for conferring some dignity on millions of human beings who are only human by name; all this certainly reflects the will of Christ. Whoever misses the bus with respect to fundamental social change is certainly going to be left by the wayside. Therefore, nothing is more necessary for Christians than to make sure they understand the social forces at work, and to try to help them in their truly formidable tasks with all the moral and intellectual resources at their command; resources which ultimately derive from the compassion of Christ and the righteousness of God.

Many a church advertising itself as preaching "the full gospel" actually preaches about one third of it. Living on a steady diet of limited evangelistic appeals, it knows little about worship and almost entirely neglects the social implications of the gospel. The evangelism of the future must go beyond a merely individualistic emphasis or cease to be taken seriously by the world. It is not enough to cry "What must I do to be saved?" A man must go on to cry "What can I do to save?"

Many other matters related to balanced, evangelistic preaching require emphasis at this point. Many are dealt with elsewhere. Some will have to be by-passed because of the limitations of space. It needs, however, to be stated that the evangelism of tomorrow must be Christocentric. "If the Church is going to make any impression on the modern mind," writes Dorothy Sayers, "she will have to preach Christ on the cross. Of late years the Church has not succeeded very well in preaching Christ: she has preached Jesus, which is not quite the same thing."

Because many have not understood Christ's deity, or have been afraid of it (or have doubted it), they have tended to fall into the preaching of mere ethical homilies rather than the Christian gospel. They argue long and earnestly for Christian principles and fail to realize that there *are* no Christian principles worth getting excited about apart from Christ. The principles so frequently exalted have little meaning in themselves; what validates them is the authority of Christ. And he has no particular authority, if he is not, as he claimed to be, deity.

It is an inescapable fact that much of the preaching in Christian pulpits is not Christian. The Bible may be the source book, the sayings of Jesus may be quoted and his life set forth in detail, the traditions of the Church may be referred to and the arguments of the Epistles may be repeated, yet the sermon is not Christian. So many sermons are frustrating appeals to better living without the slightest clue as to how those who cry with the Apostle Paul, "the good that I would, I do not; [and] the evil that I would not, that I do," can accomplish it. It is a pretty discouraging business to sit in church Sunday after Sunday and have Jesus held up as an example, to be called upon to follow him, and not have the power to do it. After a while the whole business is no longer taken seriously.

The Christian Church exists and evangelizes only as it lives in its faith in Christ's saviorhood. If he is not deity then the Church is a mere ethical society with nothing very unique to say. If the supernatural is dropped from the gospel it ceases to be the gospel. If Jesus is merely a man (albeit incomparable, transcendent, Godlike) then there is no gospel. The gospel means "good news" and, "if Christ be not risen," the record of his life and death is stunningly bad news. It means, simply, that Jesus was wrong about the nature of the universe. It means that, if there is a God at all, he is impersonal, detached, and utterly indifferent to justice, suffering, and goodness.

What validates the entire Christian message is the death and resurrection of Jesus. In this the Christian religion is unique. Christianity is not a set of ideals, although it holds to many, or a body of teaching, although the Bible encompasses a great corpus of truth; Christianity is Christ. In the strictest sense, the Bible is not the Word of God; Jesus is. *He* is what God has to say. The revelation is not conveyed by his teaching but in his person. *He* is the revelation of the nature and will of God.

The Church whose gospel is Christocentric will find itself called to preach both the goodness and severity of God. The Church will avoid sentimentality by preaching Christ. One is likely to get a sentimental view of love in the New Testament unless one gets one's view of love *from* the New Testament. In the New Testament and particularly at the cross one sees the love of God. But it is also at the cross that the judgment of God is seen. God's supreme attribute is love. There is a tendency to forget, however, that this same love makes Him inflexible in His opposition to sin. The Church has frequently sentimentalized the love of God and made it a soft and flaccid thing. The God of much preaching is all sweetness and light; not a Father in heaven but, as someone has suggested, "a Grandfather in heaven," overlooking our deliberate disobedience and planting a kiss of forgiveness upon our brow even as we resist His will. This is all very lovely, but it is also very silly, and utterly unchristian.

Nobody who has ever faced real trouble is going to react with anything but impatience to that preaching that does not deal with judgment. Talk, sentimental talk, about the love of God and the beauties of nature, and glib, easy references to the Father's love will evoke disappointment and the sense of being betrayed in the person coping with delinquent children, wrestling with his baser nature and the problems of society, or battling with incurable cancer.

There is no escaping the sterner side of the gospel. It is there, and only a blithe and irresponsible kind of wishful thinking can disregard it. It takes no very penetrating insight to see the judgment of God written into our universe and into history. The most cursory look will make it plain that the universe is designed to operate in a certain way and that not to be in harmony with it is to collide with the eternal purposes of God.

One keeps the physical "laws" or gets hurt. One keeps

the law of love in his human relationships or gets hatred and conflict. The judgment of God on imperialist exploitation and racial inequality can be seen in the growing hostility between East and West. The judgment of God upon the economic injustice of the Czarist regime in Russia was communism. The judgment of God upon crass materialism is the neurotic lostness of our society. Our international, national, and individual ills are not mere happenstance nor the vindictive retribution of a capricious deity; they are the judgment of God upon sin. To preach a bland and superficial gospel in the face of the enormous events of our time is unrealistic and unchristian.

The Church's good news in the turmoil of time is Christ. At the heart of a world under judgment stands a cross. On that cross is to be seen the love of God in full and perfect expression. At the cross we see that God is a judge, but (and this is the heartening news) the judge is a Father—*our* Father, if we will. This is no inflexible, impersonal deity, this is the God who "so loved the world" that He broke into history and revealed Himself and His will in His Son. This is the good news—that God has taken the initiative; that "God was in Christ reconciling the world to Himself."

MUCH so-called "evangelistic preaching" has been done by shoddy homileticians who gave the impression that all that is required to "do the work of an evangelist" is to string together a series of deathbed stories on a rather thin theology. But good evangelistic preaching is not the mere foisting of hackneyed clichés upon a jaded audience. Contrary to common opinion, a man is not qualified to be an evangelist simply because he possesses a set of leather lungs, an understanding of crowd psychology, and an endless supply of flamboyant illustrations.

IX.
The Goal
Is Commitment

AT THE Constituting Assembly of the World Council of Churches in Amsterdam in 1951, Stephen Neill, a Bishop of the Church of England and then Secretary of the World Council, concluded his address to the assembled ecclesiastics by leaning forward and asking simply and quietly, "How long is it since you, personally, led someone to Jesus Christ?"

Asked with like humility, the question might well be put to all Christian ministers. It is precisely for this purpose—the winning of others to Christ—that we ourselves have been won. From the grassroots to the highest echelons, from the humblest layman to the most dignified ecclesiastic, this is the Church's calling.

During the course of an evangelistic mission in a large North American city, a group of five members of the clergy were sitting about, sipping coffee, reviewing the service just concluded, and talking shop. In the midst of a discussion on evangelism one of the men interjected the remark, "I'll have to confess that if someone came to my study and asked me to help him find God, I simply wouldn't know what to do." Then, looking around at the others, he said, "And am I wrong in saying that the same would be true of all of us?" There was no demurrer.

These were cultivated and dedicated men, graduates of famous seminaries and ordained ministers in a great denomination. There was no flippancy in the statement nor was there accusation in the reference to the others. The man was simply and honestly stating his feeling of inadequacy as an evangelist. These men were not backward or unskilled; they were faithful pastors, loyal churchmen, good preachers, and skilled in liturgy. But as evangelists they were inept. Why?

There are a number of reasons for the decline in what is commonly called "evangelistic preaching"—more specifically, preaching for a verdict. One reason has already been given in the section on the failure of many theological seminaries to offer instruction in the field. There are many evangelicals who would be more "evangelistic" if they knew how to go about it. Although evangelistic preaching is not merely a matter of "techniques" the average minister needs instruction on procedure. Unfamiliarity with the mechanics of evangelistic preaching, together with the fear of blundering, has deterred many from venturing to preach for a verdict.

Moreover, preaching for a verdict has often seemed demeaning. The terminology commonly employed has been so bandied about and abused that some ministers incline to avoid any pulpit activity even remotely connected with seeking "decisions for Christ." They leave it to simpler souls. In point of fact, however, it is not a simple thing to preach a good evangelistic sermon; it is, perhaps, the most difficult kind of preaching. Much so-called "evangelistic preaching" has been done by shoddy homileticians who gave the impression that all that is required to "do the work of an evangelist" is to string together a series of deathbed stories on a rather thin theology. But good evangelistic preaching is not the mere foisting of hackneyed clichés upon a jaded audience. Contrary to common opinion, a man is not qualified to be an evangelist simply because he possesses a set of leather lungs, an understanding of crowd psychology, and an endless supply of flamboyant illustrations.

Evangelistic preaching that seeks a specific verdict is not for the irresponsible or the ill-prepared. The evangelist faces the infinitely difficult task of bringing his hearers to a place of commitment. If he has respect for human personality and is seeking more than immediate results, his task is one of the most difficult in ministry. That it has frequently been done, and with apparent success, by men who have depended principally upon bombast makes it all the more imperative that responsible evangelicals do not surrender the field.

Another reason for the decline in evangelistic preaching has been the fear of an adverse reaction. This is a grievous error. Experience has shown that most moderns do not resent candid and pointed preaching, if it is done reasonably and sympathetically. Young people welcome specifically evangelistic preaching and respond in a manner that is a humbling thing to see. The National Socialists in Germany knew something about challenge and response that the Church has often forgotten. They called millions of German youth to dedicated living and found a glad and enthusiastic response. These young people were later betrayed, but there is another kind of betrayal: the failure to call young people to commitment and devotion to Christ. There is ample evidence that this generation of young people stands ready to respond to the call to Christian discipleship. The Church must not fail to challenge them because of timidity or undue apprehension as to their reaction.

It must be understood, of course, that there *is* "the offense of the cross" to be borne by those who preach the Christian gospel with faithfulness. Man's will is at cross-purposes with God's, and where there is an unwillingness to bring one's life under the lordship of Christ there will be unconcern or rebellion. Inasmuch as Jesus provoked the most violent opposion—so violent as to come eventually to blood lust—it would be foolish to expect that his teaching can be forthrightly presented in our day and create no offense. We must expect some to recoil in unbelief and rebellion, not only because the assertions are astounding to the mind, but because the call is to the crucifixion of the ego. The faithful statement of Christ's demands (and they are totalitarian demands) will always provoke some offense. This is to be expected and is unavoidable.

However, much of the antagonism raised by the preaching of the gospel is not so much antipathy to the message as to the messenger. Not a few contend for the faith contentiously. It has been said that Whitefield, the great English evangelist, could say the word "Constantinople" in such a way as to bring tears; there have been others who could make "Mary had a little lamb" sound like a personal insult. Dwight L. Moody used to inquire of students whom he had sent out on weekend preaching engagements, "Did you make anybody mad?"—on the assumption that there would necessarily be some kind of adverse reaction to a faithful declaration of the gospel. There is some truth in this, but much room for error. What is called "the offense of the cross" is often, in fact, the offensiveness of the preacher.

A further reason for the failure to preach evangelistically is that shrinking from the personal involvement that evangelism calls for in the preacher. The man who would call others to decision must first scrutinize his own life. It is pure hypocrisy to cry "Christ can change the world" if the preacher is, himself, unchanged. He who would win others to faith must first examine his own. It is not likely that a man will preach the gospel persuasively and convincingly if he has not found the gospel effective within his own experience. George Eliot has said, "Ideas are poor things until they become incarnate."

The minister does not seek, of course, to validate the gospel by arguing from his own experience but it is probable that positive and radiant preaching will be done only by the man who has first preached to himself. At Gethsemane Jesus prayed, "For *their* sakes I sanctify *myself*." His prayer must be the prayer of the man who seeks the commitment of others. For the sake of those apart from God, for the sake of the Church and for his own sake, he must sanctify himself. A shrinking from evangelism may be a shrinking from the ordeal of coming to terms with one's own soul.

By what right does a man preach the gospel? By what right does he stand before his fellows and presume to talk about God? Is this not a superlative kind of egotism? How can the finite mind begin to comprehend the infinite God— a God whose ways are not our ways and are "past finding out"? If a man thinks he is *wise* enough to speak of God, he demonstrates that he is not good enough, for obviously he has never learned humility. If he thinks he is *good* enough to speak of God, he demonstrates that he is not wise, for obviously he has not looked deeply into his own frailties. By what right, then, does the minister speak of God? Is it because he has been to a theological seminary and studied Greek and homiletics and Church history? No, for though these are important to ministry, they are not requisite. Is it because he is a better man than those to whom he speaks? No, for he is not. On the face of it, the man who stands before his fellows and speaks of the nature and will of God appears, of necessity, either a consummate egotist or the worst kind of fool. Which indeed he would be, were it not for another factor.

Preaching is the expression of the most flagrant egotism unless the preacher is under a compulsion; unless, as a result of a divine-human encounter he "cannot *but* speak the things that [he has] seen and heard." In the final analysis preaching is a bearing of witness. The preacher speaks from a background of confrontation by God. At some point in his life (and subsequently) Deity drew near, and all that he now speaks of God is informed by and is the result of that self-revelation. The minister's faith is not merely a faint hope shored up with logic and syllogism; it is grounded in experience. His experience is not the ecstasy of the mystic, but the response to love—the love of God in Jesus Christ. This divine-human relationship is the ground of preaching. Apart from it the preacher is the ultimate egotist.

Now, to the matter of preaching for a verdict. The Christian preacher does not simply say, "This is the truth," but, "This is the truth—how will you respond to it?" Detached speculation about ethical premises may serve religion well, but not Christianity. Christianity is intensely personal. God makes demands upon men. Christian truth is not merely something to be understood; it is something to which one must respond. The preacher is preaching for a verdict.

Before he sets himself to this task, however, he must be

convinced of the power of the gospel to transform. Evangelical Christianity is the combination of the most absolute
pessimism about man's unaided powers with an unwavering
optimism as to what, by God's grace, man may become. As
Karl Barth has put it, "Without any possibility on our side
God's great possibility comes into view, making possible
what is impossible from our side." In Martin Luther's
words: "I believe that not of my own reason and power do
I believe in my Lord or am able to come to Him." The
encounter issues from God and the response is called forth
by Him.

In this conviction it is not difficult for faith to conceive
of the possibility of the radical transformation of human
personality. In point of fact this is the heart of the gospel:
That men may be changed by the power of God. Indeed, the
Christian creed can only validate itself by the production
of Christian character.

> Jesus hid within a Book
> Isn't worth a second look.
> Jesus buried in a creed,
> Is a helpless Christ indeed.
> But Jesus in the hearts of men
> Shows his saving pow'r again.

It seems clear that Jesus intended the Church to authenticate
its appeal to the world by the quality of its life. The Church
is in the world (where Jesus prayed it would remain) not to
dispute or to denounce, but to demonstrate. Creeds are im-

portant in a historic faith, and theology is requisite if Christians would maintain the relative purity of their beliefs, but these things are secondary to the witness of a redeemed society.

Evangelicals must return to the conviction that a man can be radically converted; that God is able totally to transform human personality. The phrase "totally to transform" must not be taken to mean that the person becomes totally different; it means, rather, that his basic proclivities are changed. One faces the same confusion of terms in speaking of "total depravity." "Total depravity" does not mean that man is utterly depraved; it means that he is depraved in the sum total of his faculties; that he is, in himself, incapable of any completely unselfish action or absolutely holy aspiration. To say that the gospel can effect the transformation of human personality is to say that in man's response to the gospel his life is brought under the Lordship of Christ in such a way as to change fundamentally the bent of his life toward God. His life is no longer ego-centered but now centers in God.

The man who would preach for a verdict must not only believe that God *can* transform human personality; he must expect to *see* it as a result of the proclamation of the gospel. He may expect to see dramatic demonstrations of the power of God to redeem as a result of his preaching. He must not, however, fall into the error common among the evangelistically inclined: that men are converted *only* in dramatic and cataclysmic ways. In simple fact no two people come to God in exactly the same way. To some the light comes like a bolt of lightning flashes across the sky, illumining the scene in a split second of time; to others the light comes slowly, like the dawn. Some, like Paul, enter the kingdom in a sudden about-face; the majority enter through the nurture of the Church in a gradual and growing commitment.

This is the goal of the preacher: to see transformed lives. That men may be changed is attested to in every era. All can call to mind individuals in history and in the present whose lives have been transformed by their response to God. And history can repeat itself as we preach.

It should be made clear that *all* Christian preaching seeks a verdict of some kind. This is not to suggest that there is only one kind of preaching; a faithful minister must teach, expound, inspire, interpret and discuss dozens of themes. On any Sunday morning a good pastor is many things; he is a *prophet* bringing to bear the prophetic note of the gospel and letting it stand in judgment over against our lives and our society; he is a *teacher* instructing his hearers in the mysteries of the faith; he is a *priest* leading the people in their worship. But within each of these expressions of his ministry, he is never the *evangelist*, seeking to win the non-Christian to Christ and the Christian to deeper commitment. His every duty has implicit within it the witness to the evangel, and his every sermon is at heart evangelistic.

This was true of Jesus. In every sermon he preached and in most of the conversations he held, he was seeking a verdict. To the Samaritan woman, after a discussion about the relative merits of Jerusalem and other places for worship, he spoke, not only of "living water," but the price of it—a proper marital relationship. The plain inference was, "Choose! Decide!" To Peter, after the resurrection and the early morning breakfast on the beach, he said, "Lovest thou me more than these?" If so, then choose! Decide! To the Rich Young Ruler, in response to his query how he might find eternal life, he made the issue clear: possessions or discipleship. Choose! Decide! In the Sermon on the Mount (seldom regarded as an "evangelistic" sermon) he finished with an illustration about houses and foundations, and said, "He that heareth these sayings of mine and doeth them is like a wise man. . . . He that heareth . . . and doeth them not is like a fool. . . ." Choose! Decide!

The point is that, whether implicit or explicit, in all Jesus' sermons and conversations there was a "watershed of decision." He made the issue crystal clear and set it before the individual. With no attempt to intimidate or entreat. It was the simple setting forth of the necessity for decision, after which the individual was allowed to make up his own mind. This is not to suggest that our every sermon must be technically an "evangelistic sermon," but that every sermon must—if it is Christian—bring the gospel to bear on some area of life in such a way that the issue is clear and a "watershed of decision" is created.

The Church must cease to think of evangelism as having to do only with the initial call to commitment. The lives of

Christians need to be evangelized. Every Christian has areas in his life in which he needs to be converted. One of the major weaknesses of the Church is that much of its membership is only half-converted. Christians need not only to be instructed and given opportunity for worship and service, they need to be evangelized. The Evangel is the "good news of God," and the "good news" in the matter of racial equality, for instance, is that "God hath made of one blood every nation under heaven."

The verdict sought through preaching is not necessarily a first decision. Christianity is not a matter of making a single "decision for Christ"; it is a whole life of decision. The command is to "take up thy cross daily," and one carries the cross through new territory in every stage of the Christian pilgrimage. Men must constantly be called to continual commitment and to the dedication of new areas of their lives. This too is evangelism.

The evangelical is not content merely to talk about religion or to comment on interesting facets of biblical truth. It is much easier to make of Christianity a sort of philosophy, rather than a way of life. The Christian preacher seeks a verdict; every truth he states, every argument he marshals, every illustration he employs has as its ultimate purpose the winning of an affirmative response from his hearers. He is not a scholar expounding his views or a philosopher delineating his ideas; he is an ambassador for Christ seeking to reconcile men to God.

A minister regularly preaching to his people and yet never specifically seeking to bring them to commitment, fails to fulfill his calling. Moreover he is frustrating his congregation. The World Council of Churches at Amsterdam described evangelism as "so making Christ known to men that each is confronted with the necessity of a personal decision, Yes or No." It is the sin of evasion that keeps great numbers from God, and the minister who speaks of the Christian way of life without ever giving specific instructions how to enter upon it, or who fails to provide an opportunity to do so is merely helping to deepen the already ingrained habit of procrastination. Persons do not just gravitate into the life of fellowship with God; they must choose. The gospel is an imperative, not an extra. Culture and virtue are not enough; the gospel is literally a matter of life and death.

And it is not as though the matter of decision may be held in abeyance. To make no choice is to choose. If you don't choose to grow flowers, you choose weeds. Life is based upon choice; by volition or by neglect. There is a principle at the heart of life: life is not what you find, it is what you create. Man is born with two things: existence and opportunity; and these are the raw materials out of which, under God, he can create a worth-while life. He is given the gift of time; he can choose to use it or to waste it. He is given a brain; he can choose to develop it or to let it stagnate. He is given human companionship; he can choose to live in harmony or in strife. Life is based upon choice, and there is no avoiding it.

Hence, the minister, dealing as he does with the central choice in life, cannot be content to speak vaguely about the necessity for commitment. As James Black has said, "Our business is serious gunfire with a target." Too much Christian preaching is like sheet lightning—it is general. It was said of one minister that he had "the art of *almost* saying something." This is not to suggest that there must be the labored pointing of a moral, or a public invitation at the end of each discourse; it means, simply, that, whether evident or implicit, the call to commitment is essential to Christian preaching.

THE GREATEST danger the evangelistic preacher faces is the danger of "success." Having had some apparent effectiveness with a particular approach or technique, he tends to baptize the method, make it standard practice, and fall into the sin of professionalism. Subsequently, his efforts in evangelism degenerate into a pattern, and he begins to manipulate personality through the use of increasingly perfected techniques. Visible results assume greater importance, and an increasing unconcern for the sacredness and inviolability of personality becomes evident. People become digits to be totted up on an adding machine as an indication of the "results" of evangelistic effort.

X.
Reckoning with the Emotions

IT IS impossible to deal properly with evangelistic preaching without giving consideration to the emotional content of the sermon. It is at this point that the Church has fallen into extremes. There are those who have been given to excessive emotionalism, wreaking havoc in personality and bringing a reproach on all evangelism. At the other extreme are those who have sought studiously to eschew emotion in the presentation of the gospel and have turned Christianity into a mere ethical culture. Both extremes are wrong.

The history of evangelism is replete with instances of rampant emotionalism. In frontier times in America, widespread manifestations of quaking, jerking, weeping, and prostration accompanied evangelistic preaching. In many cases, penitents fell into a trancelike state and lay in a condition not far removed from suspended animation for lengthy periods. This condition, described as "slain of the Lord," is still occasionally seen in "holiness" and pentecostal circles. Itinerant evangelists frequently made deliberate attempts to work on the emotions of their hearers till a great deal of shouting and running about took place. To this day, in some of the smaller denominations, an evangelist's effectiveness is often reckoned by his ability to provoke an audible and sometimes physical response.

It must not be thought that all the early American revivalists encouraged emotional excess. To the contrary. Charles G. Finney, for instance, took particular pains to avoid any emotional display in his services and would dismiss the after-service at the first sign of audible weeping or uncontrolled emotion. Nevertheless, Finney's autobiography relates many instances where the extreme manifestations common to that day were in evidence.

In more recent years many itinerant evangelists have deliberately played upon the emotions of their hearers to achieve their immediate end—a large response to the invitation. Most modern evangelists of any reputation play down the emotional aspects of their ministry and even make statements warning of the dangers. The repudiation of emotionalism does not mean, however, that the evangelist does not employ a strong emotional appeal, even though unwittingly. Disclaimers to the contrary, the content of the sermon and the manipulative techniques used to effect a response are vitally emotional in character. The appeal to fear, the hypnotic effect of sustained, rapid-fire preaching, the soft insinuating music of the commonly used invitation hymns, the importunities of the "personal workers," and the "electric" mood of the service, exert an appeal that is difficult for most and impossible for some to resist.

This must not be construed to mean that emotional content should be absent in preaching. On the contrary, good evangelism makes an appeal to the whole man—emotions, intellect, and will. The preacher must speak to the emotions, but must be careful that the hearer's judgment is not beclouded by his feelings; he must speak to the intellect, but be ever mindful that Christianity is more than the mere acceptance of certain propositions about God; he must always, finally, speak to the will and win his hearers to a volitional response.

Of the inordinate fear of emotion that has stultified a great segment of the Church, more will be said later. Let a word be said now about the need for sensitivity and good taste in that pointed preaching of the gospel which seeks a verdict. It is well to be anxious for the souls of men and zealous to claim them for the Kingdom, but there is a "zeal without knowledge" of which the Bible warns. Many volatile persons are carried away with themselves and their message and become insufferable boors. The man seeking a verdict is on holy ground and must not profane it by graceless and intemperate pleas. Many have been prejudiced against the Christian faith by preachers who seem to feel that their faithfulness is measured by the length and tenacity of their appeal. An insensitive and prolonged appeal frequently wins nothing but resentment. There is a story about an old lady in a poor parish who summed up the feeling of many when she said to her minister, "I don't want any of those evangelist fellows comin' 'round here savin' my soul on me!"

There are two principal dangers in the evangelism characterized by emotionalism: first, it tends to induce a counterfeit Christian experience and a consequently unbalanced approach to the Christian life, second, the decision effected while the individual is overwrought emotionally may eventually be injurious to mental health. The predominantly emotional religious experience usually creates an initial sense of assurance later belied by the facts. As a result of this pendulum swing, the "convert" is confused and usually turns to one of two extremes: he seeks to duplicate the initial experience and launches upon an emotionally conditioned religious life, or he feels that he has been betrayed and subsequently regards all religious experience with suspicion.

The fact is that many of the "converts" of churches whose evangelism is characterized by emotion-centered appeals have never been caused to face up to what is involved in Christian experience. They merely pass through what might be termed an "emotional catharsis." The problem arises from an improper emphasis by the preacher. Much contemporary evangelism consists of the denunciation of specific sins and the announcement of forgiveness. This oversimplified and negative approach to the problem of sin induces a sense of guilt in the hearer. Stimulated by this sense of guilt (usually related to some particular reprehensible acts in his past) the hearer responds, is prayed with, given assurances of pardon, and told that, as a result of his willingness to "accept Jesus Christ as his personal Savior," he has become a Christian. At this point he usually experiences a feeling of release which he interprets as the evidence of God's presence in forgiveness. Subsequently, the "convert" is drawn into the life of the Church.

It is unfortunate that this kind of thing should happen (as it does thousands of times annually in Fundamentalist circles), not only because the "convert" has been seriously misled, but because the experience he has undergone is not a "Christian" experience and, indeed, may be the very thing to bar him from a genuine relationship with God. It is an experience akin to that of the offender against the law who turns himself in and volitionally confesses his crime. Almost invariably he follows his confession by a statement to the effect: "Oh, it feels good to get that off my chest!" He feels a sense of release, of relative well-being. This "emotional catharsis" is of the same nature and is brought about by a similar set of circumstances as the feeling of release and "forgiveness" felt by the individual who has come forward and confessed his sins in an evangelistic service where the emphasis has been such as to heighten the sense of guilt for specific past misdeeds.

The problem grows out of the preacher's failure to under-

stand the nature of sin and the ground of Christian commitment. He is under the impression that he is preaching on
"sin" when, in fact, he has been preaching on "sins"—the
acts growing out of the basic "sin." The sin of which a man
must be convicted, if he is to be led to God, is the sin of
pride; the sin of self-sufficiency, that alienation of the self
from God in which the individual arrogates to himself lordship over his own life. The man who is merely brought to
the confession of certain reprehensible acts in his past and
not made to realize that it is not so much his past which
needs forgiveness as his self-will, will have failed to face
up to the prerequisite of Christian experience—the bringing
of one's life under the Lordship of Christ. As a result there
will be no significant change in his life. The ego remains
untouched; the "old man" still lives and rules.

This failure to make clear the central issue at the heart
of Christian commitment is the reason for the constant
schism in the so-called "evangelistic" churches. Converts
are called to "an experience in Christ" (which is often non-
Christian) and subsequently taken into the church. But the
new member's basic character is not changed; he has merely
changed context. Deeply lodged resentments and hostilities
must now find new outlets and frequently evidence themselves in the criticism of other Christians, attacks upon
what are rather ambiguously called "modernists," and
general disagreement with those who worship and believe differently. This "baptized egotism," so often the
result of bad evangelism, is responsible for the constant

schism over doctrine in evangelistically inclined sects.

The minister who plays upon the emotions of his hearers denies God's creativity. His anti-intellectualism is the refusal to obey the great commandment to "love God with the whole mind." He confuses faith with credulity and labors under the false notion that God is pleased with zeal apart from knowledge.

He is guilty, further, of the sin of sloth. Having found that he can accomplish the desired response in his hearers by playing upon their emotions, he takes the easy way and effects his end without troubling to discipline his mind or examine his results. Moreover, he is not usually content to pursue such a course for himself, but manages to convince himself that his is the ideal way and that those approaching the task more thoughtfully are guilty of some kind of compromise with what he chooses to call "the truth." Not infrequently he will come to be suspicious of anything even remotely cerebral.

There is a familiar story relating how John Wesley, a university-trained man, received a note from a self-appointed "evangelist" informing him that "the Lord has told me to tell you that He doesn't need your book learning; your Greek and your Hebrew." Wesley replied, "Thank you, sir. Your letter was superfluous, however, as I already knew the Lord has no need for my 'book-learning,' as you put it. However —although the Lord hasn't directed me to say so—on my own responsibility I would say to you that the Lord doesn't need your ignorance either."

The great weakness of an emotionally based evangelism is that it limits the gospel. It limits its outreach, finding its response among the relatively illiterate and having little to say to intellectuals. It limits the very gospel itself, confining its statement to particular facets of the Christian message and neglecting many of the great emphases. So much of this kind of evangelism is 10 per cent statement and 90 per cent appeal; in the New Testament the proportions would be reversed.

There is, however, another side to this matter of the emotional content in evangelism requiring emphasis. In a great segment of the Church there is an inordinate fear of emotion. Uncontained emotion being repugnant, some have withdrawn to the opposite extreme and have almost eliminated the emotional content from their preaching. Some have so "Hellenized" the gospel that they will suffer anything rather than emotion—even boredom!

How far removed much of our contemporary preaching is from the New Testament and the great hours of Christian history! How unlike Jesus we are in our carefully ordered and dispassionate statement of the gospel! See him with fire in his eye and anger in his voice denouncing the Pharisees; watch him as, with whip of cords in his hand, he drives men and animals alike from the temple; hear him weep over the unyielding city and sense the passion throbbing in his voice as he cries out against those who exploited the poor and the dispossessed. How little we know of the fire that blazed in Paul's spirit and made him to exclaim his desire to win his brethren even at the cost of his own soul. Listen to Peter as he shouts, "We cannot but speak the things we have seen and heard"; to Stephen as he breathes that dread indictment of the enemies of the cause of which he was enthralled; to Savonarola's thundering denunciations; to Luther's adamant statement of his conviction! Call the roll of the great preachers, and they have been men of enormous passion. True, there were other factors at the heart of their usefulness; but these men moved the world around them, stirred their hearers, and bequeathed a heritage that still lives, through the throbbing intensity of their passion.

The Church tends to fear the emotions. Because of the excesses committed in the past and still perpetrated today, the thoughtful minister often avoids any emphasis or manner of presentation that might conceivably come under suspicion of being overemotional. As a result, much preaching is as dry as dust. It is intelligent and well stated and yields evidence of the most painstaking preparation, but it is "flat, stale and unprofitable." And it betrays an abysmal ignorance of human nature. We are in serious error if we are under the illusion that the majority is moved by logic. The cleverly oriented and exhaustive study of any theme is, in logical presentation, fascinating to the scholar, but the fact is it leaves the so-called "average man" cold. He is moved and comes to most of his conclusions through his emotions. (Indeed, a strong case could be made for the assertion that even "intellectuals" are influenced in their major choices more by emotion than by logic.)

The Church must not fear emotion; it must seek to understand it. Emotion is basic to life. Love is an emotion, as is hate and fear and joy. Our response to many of the arts is almost entirely emotional in character. Many a dignified liturgist who decries the evangelist's use of emotion to accomplish his ends, fails to realize that he too is designedly making an emotional impress upon his congregation through the great vaulting arches and the hushed, insulated quiet of the sanctuary. The emotions are the great driving forces in life. Skillful logic is often wasted, for many do not think logically. Appeals to the will are often fruitless, for many are constitutionally indecisive and unable to make up their minds about anything. Emotion, judiciously used by the minister aware of the dangers involved, may be the catalyst needed to precipitate a Christian decision.

Let no one think that emotion can be separated from religion. There is not, of course, so much danger that the "old-line churches" will fall into rampant emotionalism as that they will entirely avoid it. Too many times we have made dignity and order the supreme virtues. (Significantly, funerals are dignified occasions while weddings and births are usually filled with emotion.) That the individual, the nation, and the world should be called to repentance and the life with God in totally dispassionate tones is as difficult to conceive as the picture of a lover announcing his devotion to his beloved in the same flat tones with which he asks his barber for a haircut.

Winston Churchill's wartime speeches are the perfect secular example of a properly balanced appeal. When Britain stood alone against the Nazis he broadcast a call for firm resolve and courageous dedication. He informed the mind and challenged the will, but, more importantly, he made you *feel!* As a consequence the British people faced their "greatest hour" with a matchless spirit. Much evangelical preaching is mature in content and precise in statement, but leaves the hearer cold. There is a note of urgency in the evangel and, if it is missing from the proclamation, the gospel seems unconvincing. We preach a total gospel to the total man—emotions, intellect, and will—and, while care must be taken never to presume upon the mind or volition through deliberate stimulation of the emotions, the gospel is not properly preached if the proclamation is devoid of passion. Unamuno, the great Spanish philosopher, has an appropriate word for the evangelical:

> *Hay que ser locos,*
> *Pero no tontos.*

Let us be crazy, but not stupid!

Many evangelicals have been hesitant to engage in the practice of evangelism through the fear instilled by a smattering of psychiatry that they may inflict injury upon the personality of their hearers. The danger is real and needs to be recognized. Negative, denunciatory preaching can heighten an abnormal sense of guilt, and a narrow, legalistic approach to the gospel can produce a hypersensitive conscience and abnormal inhibitions. But it is a grave misunderstanding of both the Christian gospel and the laws of mental health to suppose that balanced and pointed evangelistic preaching is deleterious to personality.

The contrary view is put forth by Dr. Leslie D. Weatherhead in his book, *Psychology, Religion and Healing:* "The forgiveness of God is the most powerful therapeutic idea in the world." And Dr. James S. Stewart has written "Who can tell the incalculable results of the words of absolution for the integration of human personalities? Who can say how many demons are being exorcised, how many potentialities of mental trouble, neurasthenia and even organic disease are rooted out by the assurance of pardon and renewal?"

Admittedly both men are Christian ministers, but their general sentiments echo in the views of many of the great psychiatrists. Psychiatry and Christianity are not incompatible; rather, they supplement each other. Psychiatry is principally negative; Christianity is principally positive. A prominent American psychiatrist has said, "Psychiatry can untangle the twisted skein of a man's affairs, but it offers no new pattern for the reweaving." A psychoanalyst attached to the Kansas State Mental Hospital observed to the writer: "As a psychoanalyst I am chiefly concerned to uncover and cause to be released the conflicts and tensions buried in the unconscious. My work is amoral. As a psychoanalyst, I have achieved my goal when my patient is symptom-free." It is precisely where psychiatry finishes that Christianity begins and provides the dynamic for positive, purposeful living. There are no rules for mental health comparable to the teachings of Jesus, and no power to fulfill the highest demands of life apart from God.

The average minister dare not lay claim to skill in psychotherapy and should take heed lest he let a little knowledge in this field become a dangerous thing. Though his counseling often parallels the work of the psychiatrist and is not infrequently successful where psychotherapy has failed, he must exercise every caution lest he fall into quackery and do great harm. The Christian minister ought not to be intimidated by the psychiatrist, but he must be aware of the great contributions to the understanding of human behavior made by these men who plumb the nether regions of the mind. He needs a sufficient understanding of psychiatry's basic premises to enable him to recognize and refer for professional treatment the victim of the more severe neuroses. He needs an acute awareness of the fact that mental illness can block the individual from true Christian conversion, that some types of so-called "Christian experience" are evidence of mental disorder and that certain approaches to preaching can be exceedingly dangerous to the disturbed.

Beyond this, however, is the assurance of the tremendous contribution the gospel can make in the lives of many people who are neurotic through, in part, a lack of purpose or unresolved feelings of guilt within their lives. Dr. C. J. Jung in *Modern Man in Search of a Soul* indicates how relevant the Christian faith may be. He writes, "Among all my patients

in the second half of life—those over thirty-five—there has
not been one whose problem in the last resort was not that
of finding a religious outlook on life. It is safe to say that
every one of them fell ill because he had lost that which the
living religions of every age have given to their followers;
and none of them has been really healed who did not regain
his religious outlook."

That evangelical preaching which specifically seeks a
verdict must always be predicated upon the sovereignty of
God. Men are to be won by what is described as "the
foolishness of preaching," but it would be foolish to hope to
win individuals to the Christian way of life by preaching
alone. The preacher must ever be conscious that it is the
operation of the Spirit of God in human life which trans-
forms his dying words into eternal instruments and uses them
to fashion the souls of men. Any effectiveness he may have
is born of God's entreaties within the consciousness of the
hearer. We do not call men to God in ourselves: "No man
cometh to the Father," said Jesus, "except my Spirit draw
him."

There is no lesson to be learned by the evangelist so important as this. He must always be conscious that men and
women are not won simply by skill or persuasiveness. "Not
by might, not by power, but by my Spirit," says the divine
word. Here the preacher learns humility. Here, too, he
learns to respect human personality. The greatest sin in
evangelism is that thoughtless, professional tampering with
the souls of men which has so often characterized it. God

Himself will not violate a man's will, but not infrequently evangelists blunder with muddied feet into this sacred place to effect their own purposes.

Let this be stated as axiomatic in the practice of evangelism: decisions must never be effected through deliberate coercion. A preacher may plead, he may argue, he may entreat and persuade, but he may never coerce. Let no one justify the winning of a response by psychological or emotional pressure on the ground of his "love for souls"; Jesus loved with "an everlasting love," yet he would not coerce.

Look, for instance, at his dealing with the Rich Young Ruler. After the young man had stated that he had kept the commandments "from his youth up" and had inquired further as to what was required of him that he might find eternal life, Jesus bade him sell his possessions, distribute them to the poor and come and follow him. The young man, as the record states, "went away sorrowfully, for he had great possessions." Here is the invitation given and a negative response. Now what? Many a contemporary evangelist would have hastened after the young man to tug on his sleeeve and entreat him to "believe." Others might try to intimidate him with dire predictions concerning his future if he persisted in his refusal. What did Jesus do? He watched him go and said (to paraphrase): "How hard it is for those who put their trust in other things to enter into the Kingdom of heaven."

Jesus never coerced. He put the issue clearly before the

individual and then left him to make up his mind as to his response. This is the task of the Christian evangelist: to present the issues at the heart of the Christian faith in lucid, unequivocal terms, and then to provide opportunity for decision. The issue must never be confused by a deliberate stirring of the emotions. In the final analysis the decision is made in the will, and the minister must never pressure his hearers into ill-considered or premature commitment.

It must clearly be understood that all who hear a sermon on Christian commitment are not, as a consequence, automatically ready to yield their wills to God. There is a "fullness of time" in every life, and it is the vanity of the preacher to believe that everyone present has sufficient "light" to make a decision simply because he (the preacher) has delivered himself of his "Royal George." It is an indication of an abysmal ignorance and a revelation of spiritual pride to presume that a city, a congregation, or an individual is bound to respond simply because we have preached to them.

All preaching does not lead to immediate commitment. Though his goal is a verdict for Christ, the preacher must often be content merely to kindle a spark within the life of some of his hearers—a spark that may kindle to flame months or years later. Commitment is seldom, if ever, the result of a single impress. Dozens of people and dozens of circumstances have previously made a contribution to the total impact of the Spirit of God upon the life of the individual who now responds.

There is a sense in which conversion is *never* instantaneous; it is always the result of a process. The conversion experience may be instantaneous or may not, but it comes into being as the result of who knows how many circumstances welded together by God. In the final analysis the individual is won to God by God Himself. All preaching as such is vain and is indeed "foolishness" apart from the operation of His Spirit. The purpose of an evangelistic sermon is to say the thing that will enable the Spirit of God to "preach" to a quickened consciousness.

The greatest danger the evangelistic preacher faces is the danger of "success." Having had some apparent effectiveness with a particular approach or technique, he tends to baptize the method, make it standard practice, and fall into the sin of professionalism. Subsequently, his efforts in evangelism degenerate into a pattern, and he begins to manipulate personality through the use of increasingly perfected techniques. Visible results assume greater importance, and an increasing unconcern for the sacredness and inviolability of personality becomes evident. People become digits to be totted up on an adding machine as an indication of the "results" of evangelistic effort.

The evangelistic preacher must remain sensitive to the fact that he is dealing with men and women for whom Christ died, and the greater his effectiveness the more he stands in danger of destroying his usefulness through professionalism.

THE PREACHER who presses God's demands upon others must needs make great demands upon himself. To stand upon the threshold of a person's life and speak pointedly to the deeps of his spirit calls for the utmost delicacy of good taste and sympathetic understanding.

XI.

The Invitation

THAT PREACHING which seeks a verdict comes inevitably to the invitation. To preach for a verdict and then fail to provide opportunity for commitment or for counsel is to frustrate one's congregation and deepen the habit of procrastination. The normal reluctance to press for decision lest some will be led to respond prematurely must be balanced against the fear that failure to give an opportunity for decision may keep others from something for which they are ready. Facing momentous decisions, we are all given to procrastination, emulating Felix in postponing decision until "a more convenient season." The invitation, in whatever way it may be given, is the normal and necessary outgrowth of evangelical preaching.

The preacher who presses God's demands upon others must needs make great demands upon himself. To stand upon the threshold of a person's life and speak pointedly to the deeps of his spirit calls for the utmost delicacy of good taste and sympathetic understanding. If he would do so, the preacher must ever keep before him a fresh consciousness of his own sinfulness or he will tend to think of himself as one who stands *above* the people calling them to repentance rather than one who stands *with* them, himself "a sinner." D. T. Niles has said that "Evangelism is one beggar telling another beggar where to find bread." The preacher has no virtue in himself. He is no paragon recommending his own way of life, but a fallible, sinful man bearing witness to God's revelation of Himself in Jesus Christ.

Too frequently the preacher fails to identify himself with his people. He speaks of "the sins of mankind" as though they are something utterly foreign to him. He talks of "man's dilemma" as though he is apart from it; as though he has not contributed to it. The preacher must never forget that the world's avarice is, in part, his avarice; its lust is his lust; its selfishness is his selfishness; its prejudices and antagonisms are his. The minister must remain constantly sensitive to his kinship with his people in their weaknesses, sins, and temptations, or fall into spiritual pride and that easy denunciation to which so many evangelists are given. He must echo the words of the Apostle Paul: "This is a faithful saying . . . that Christ Jesus came into the world to save sinners, of which *I am* chief!"

It is a fact that the minister is (in a proper understanding of the term) the greatest "sinner" in the church he serves, for the greatest sinner is always the greatest saint. The condemned murderer in his cell may know little of sin, being sensitive only to the wrong of the grossest crimes, but the saint, with his sensitivity to God's holiness and his awareness of the enormity of man's sin, knows the measure of his own "coming short." He is conscious of his own sinfulness and of the hopelessness of his condition apart from the grace of God, and in this knowledge he learns humility. In this humility he learns the implications for preaching of the doctrine of the incarnation—that identification with mankind requisite to compassionate evangelism.

Personally prepared to press the Christian demand for commitment upon his hearers, the minister comes to the point where he must provide the opportunity for response. The invitation may be given in an infinite variety of ways. There is no ideal method, and none should adopt any particular "technique" without careful consideration of all the factors involved. The bane of much evangelism in the past has been the adoption of a fixed technique and then superimposing it upon every situation. A sensitive minister, impelled by a genuine concern to help others make a profound commitment to Christ, will do with the problem of method as a hen does with an egg—brood over it until something hatches. He will study the situation in which he labors until he finds ways that will provide opportunity without violating personality.

Over the years a great many preachers have devised a great many ways of providing public opportunity for commitment. The early Church regularly responded to the articulated or implicit question, "What must we do?" by commanding the people to repent, be baptized, receive the Holy Spirit, and be added to the Church. Apparently, instruction was usually given, and the converts were entered into the Christian community. One thing is clear: the call to commitment was also a call to a relationship to the Church as "one under instruction." The early church knew nothing of the contemporary call to commitment apart from a church relationship. Such as repented were "added to the Church."

There are two basic approaches to the invitation from which all the varieties have stemmed. For convenience they may be described as the John Wesley method and the Charles G. Finney method.

John Wesley and the early Methodists popularized what has come to be called "the altar call"—a prolonged invitation to respond by coming forward, interspersed with the singing of hymns of invitation. Frequently, in early Methodism, the preacher would give way to an "exhorter" (often a layman) who would importune the congregation to respond. Those who did, moved to the front of the sanctuary (or meeting house) to kneel at what was termed a "mourner's bench"—usually the front pew or bench. There they were prayed with and counseled.

The "altar call" was sometimes extended to great length, many invitation hymns being sung and each verse being preceded by a prolonged exhortation to respond. Not infrequently the invitation was longer than the sermon—quite a tribute to the patience of the congregation and the lungs of the exhorter in a day when sermons with as many as fifteen to twenty "points" were not uncommon.

The method found great favor in the United States among early Methodists and other evangelicals, and in subsequent years was adopted, with some changes, by many American revivalists. While generally abandoned by the Methodist and other "old-line" churches today, it is still commonly used by itinerant evangelists and in some of the smaller denominations. Many refinements have been added.

In the modern form, the invitation to come forward is not given immediately at the close of the sermon, but preceded by a series of steps, through which "the sinner" is brought to an increasing degree of response. First, all present are asked to bow their heads and close their eyes. This is usually followed by the request to indicate any number of "needs" by an upraised hand. All who raise their hands are subsequently asked to stand as indication of their sincerity. Then all standing are requested to come forward that they may be prayed for. After these have responded, the "altar call" begins and, with all standing, an invitation hymn (or hymns) is sung, and others are urged to join those who have already responded.

Usually the evangelist's appeal is based upon questionable motivation: the fear of death, the rewards of the life to come, the memory of a beloved parent ("Tell Mother I'll Be There"), or any other motivation that occurs to the

evangelist. In many cases the "altar call" has little relationship to the preceding sermon. The evangelist may speak to
a different theme each night, but the appeals for decision
will usually be identical. "Personal workers" frequently move
through the congregation, making individual appeals to
supplement the general appeal. The pressure to respond is
frequently enormous—so much so that the constitutionally
irresolute often come forward every night of the mission.

It is the writer's opinion that, in the regular services of
the church, the public "altar call" is no longer a useful
device. It yields some undoubted benefits—it calls upon the
individual to take a stand for his faith and oftentimes produces great assurance—but the objections to it seem to out-
weigh the benefits. The element of coercion is usually
present; the irresolute respond to the preacher rather than
to the importunities of the Holy Spirit; the emotional tide
runs inordinately high, and many who might otherwise be
won simply refuse to respond in a manner they regard as
unseemly. It is unfortunate but true that some in rejecting
the method feel they have rejected God and are subsequently
afflicted with unnecessary remorse or despair. The method
may serve some itinerant evangelists, but as a method for use
in the regular services of the Church it is unsuitable.

Charles G. Finney devised a different approach to the
problem of the invitation and after-service. A lawyer prior
to the dramatic conversion experience that led him into the
ministry, he came to place great emphasis on volitional
response. Though his ministry was frequently accompanied

by dramatic emotional manifestations, he specifically sought to avoid emotional excess, almost to an extreme. His preaching was ordered and logical, and his appeal was directed to the will of the listener. Finney would conclude the preaching portion of the service by asking those who were "anxious about the state of their souls" to come forward and sit in what was termed "the anxious seat"—the front row or rows in the place of meeting. If the congregation was large, Finney would sometimes designate a nearby church as the place to which the "seekers" should repair. After the response he would pronounce the benediction and proceed to instruct and pray with those who had come forward. Finney's method, continued since his time, is perpetuated today in the so-called after-service.

Across the years a number of evangelical clergymen have sought to discover ways of giving opportunity for commitment. Many effective pastors have demonstrated great and useful skills in this matter. Charles Spurgeon, the great Baptist pastor in London, England, would conclude the service by announcing that the Deacons would be available in a nearby room to counsel spiritually with any who might wish to commit their lives to Christ. There were few Sundays when there was no response. Baptists have frequently invited "seekers" to come forward and present themselves to the Deacons at the front of the sanctuary to the end that they might be prayed with, baptized, and received into the church. Many variations of this general approach have been employed.

By and large ministers have turned away from the "altar call" and many are at a loss as to how to proceed. In an attempt to provide some guidance to churches that may wish to offer public opportunity for commitment, the following methods are listed. They are designed for use in the regular services of the church.

THE PRAYER OF COMMITMENT

In the Order of Worship, following the sermon, list the item, "Prayer of Commitment." Immediately at the close of the sermon, state that there will now be a brief period of silence during which each member of the congregation is asked to review his life in terms of the sermon just preached. After at least thirty seconds of silence, the minister should state that he is going to lead in a prayer of commitment and ask each person present to repeat the prayer silently as he (the minister) speaks it aloud. He should then lead in a carefully prepared prayer, in which he articulates for the congregation such statements of dedication as may have been called forth by the sermon. The prayer will be, of course, conditioned by the specific emphases of the sermon which has preceded it. Following this the closing hymn is sung, and the benediction given. Special care should be taken to see that the words of the hymn are related to the affirmations just made.

THE RESPONSIVE PRAYER OF COMMITMENT

This variation of the above differs only in that the congregation is asked to repeat responsively each phrase of a prayer as they are led in it by the minister. A caution should be uttered to the effect that none should repeat any statement in the prayer which they do not believe to be true or do not intend to fulfill. The following is an example of a responsive prayer of commitment.

Heavenly Father,
    I come to Thee because I believe in Thee.
    I believe Thou dost love the world.
    I believe Thou didst send Thy Son to die for the world.
    I believe He died for me.
    I confess my sins to Thee.
    I have done things I ought not to have done;
    Father, forgive me.
    I have left undone things I ought to have done;
    Father, forgive me.
    Help me to forsake my sins.
    I accept Jesus Christ as my Savior and Lord.
    I purpose to live for Him from this moment forward.
    Give me the faith to trust Thee.
    Give me the grace to be strong.
    Give me the courage to be true.
    In Jesus' name. Amen.

THE AFTER-SERVICE

On particular Sundays (usually not every week nor less

freauently than once a quarter) the minister might announce that, at the close of the service, there will be an after-service during which he will explain in simple, layman's language precisely what it means to be a committed Christian. (The nature of the after-service should be made crystal clear in order to avoid misunderstanding and to minimize the suspicion that those who remain are to be singled out and made subject to some kind of duress. Candor in the announcement of the after-service is essential.)

The congregation should be dismissed with the benediction as usual, and the minister should remain in the pulpit. The congregation should be informed before the benediction that those who are leaving are asked to go quickly and quietly and to forego any customary conversation in the sanctuary or the narthex. Those who wish to remain are asked to remain in their seats and then to fill in the front pews after the press of those leaving has lessened. The after-service may be announced for a nearby chapel or assembly room, but it is best to remain in the sanctuary.

As soon as silence has been established the minister should lead in a prayer and then, in simple straightforward language, clearly explain what is involved in Christian commitment. Following this the group should be led in a prayer of commitment (see above "The Responsive Prayer of Commitment"), and scriptural assurances offered.

It is recommended that literature be given to those who remain for the after-service. A portion of the Scriptures might be given, along with such other materials as may be judged helpful. It may be desired to have those present sign a decision card.

COMMITMENT THROUGH PASTORAL COUNSEL

At the close of a sermon specifically dealing with the necessity for Christian decision, the minister may state that any wishing to receive more specific counsel on the matter of their relationship to God should fill out the card placed in the pew for this purpose, or should so indicate to the minister at the door at the close of the service. When concern is indicated the minister should then make a specific appointment to visit the person or to have the person come to his study for counsel. At this time more personal assistance and guidance can be given.

COMMITMENT THROUGH CARDS IN THE PEWS

Decision cards specifically outlining a profession of faith and allowing space for a signature may be placed in the pews. At the close of a sermon calling for a decision for Christ, attention should be directed to the cards and all desirous of confessing their faith should be asked to repeat the confession with the minister, sign the card, and turn it in to the ushers or the minister when leaving. Subsequently the minister or members of the session should offer personal counsel, instruction, and such literature as may be deemed useful.

THE "ALTAR CALL"

At the close of the service an invitation should be given to come forward during the closing hymn as an expression of willingness to make a decision for Christ. Those who come forward should be asked to stand at the front of the sanctuary and, after a prayer has been offered, should be directed to the chapel, the pastor's study, or any other suitable place where they may be personally dealt with by the minister or others appointed to this task.

Those who come forward may be met by members of the session who will accompany them to the place of the after-meeting.

OTHER METHODS

In addition to the foregoing methods there is a considerable variety of other ways by which public opportunity for commitment may be provided.

(A) Those ready to live the Christian life may be asked to join a communicant's class.

(B) During the Ritual of Friendship the minister may ask all who wish to make a profession of faith and join the Church to indicate this on the Registration card.

(C) During a baptism service or prior to the Lord's Supper a public invitation to confess Christ may be given.

(D) On other occasions persons may be asked to stand momentarily as an evidence of their desire to become Christians.

(E) In some sections of the country where tradition expects it, an "altar call," during which an invitation hymn is sung, may be used.

It is essential that a clear differentiation be made between the decision to live the Christian life and the decision to unite with the Christian Church. One should follow upon the other, but they are not identical, and the distinction should be made clear.

The faithful minister who will carefully and prayerfully prepare to preach for a verdict and to provide an opportunity publicly to make a commitment to Christ will be rewarded by the knowledge that he has been used to help others to respond to God and to become heir to all the attendant blessings which grow out of this relationship.

Set in Linotype Times Roman
Format by James T. Parker
Manufactured by The Haddon Craftsmen, Inc.
Published by HARPER & BROTHERS, *New York*